MANAGEMENT AND MYTHS

MANAGEMENT
AND MYTHS

Challenging business fads, fallacies and fashions

Adrian Furnham

First published 2004 by
PALGRAVE MACMILLAN
Houndmills, Basingstoke, Hampshire RG21 6XS and
175 Fifth Avenue, New York, N.Y. 10010
Companies and representatives throughout the world

PALGRAVE MACMILLAN is the global academic imprint of the Palgrave Macmillan division of St. Martin's Press, LLC and of Palgrave Macmillan Ltd. Macmillan® is a registered trademark in the United States, United Kingdom and other countries. Palgrave is a registered trademark in the European Union and other countries.

ISBN 1–4039–2204–7

This book is printed on paper suitable for recycling and made from fully managed and sustained forest sources.

A catalogue record for this book is available from the British Library.

A catalog record for this book is available from the Library of Congress.

Editing and origination by Aardvark Editorial, Mendham, Suffolk

10 9 8 7 6 5 4 3 2 1
13 12 11 10 09 08 07 06 05 04

Printed and bound in Great Britain by
Creative Print & Design (Wales), Ebbw Vale

For A and B: you see

Contents

Introduction

The modern manager is spoilt for choice when it comes to advice on how to do a better job. The morning snail mail is often bursting with publishers' blurbs on the latest 'must have' blockbuster management book, which offers a new miracle cure for the intractable problems of management. The email also now bombards us with books, conferences, seminars and workshops on the latest, state-of-the-art thinking in management.

All the media dedicate a significant amount of line to management issues. There are dedicated radio and television programmes as well as daily newspaper columns that deal with little else. Specialist magazines also hope to satiate this unquenchable thirst for management ideas. And compared with other worlds, the 'time to market' for ideas in business and management seems particularly impressive. Why? No doubt because management is difficult and all managers want the miracle cure.

So the management world is highly susceptible to crazes: fads and fashions that change as frequently as clothes styles. And, like clothes styles, come back again after 'a few years' away – repackaged, rebranded but essentially the same. Worse, fallacious concepts are found in abundance in management. These are usually processes that simply do not work in the way they are said to. Brainstorming is a good example. Study after study shows that individuals working alone produce both more and better ideas than brainstorming groups. Brainstorming is a fallacy or a myth. But only one of many because of the essential non- or at least pre-scientific nature of management theory.

Consider each of these issues in turn.

Fads in management

A fad is a craze for something: a short time when there is an exaggerated zeal for a particular idea or practice. Fads are by definition short-lived. They go in one era and out the other. Toy manufacturers know that toy preferences are notoriously faddish. Despite their best efforts at market research some toys simply flop while others become spectacularly successful. There can be a massive demand that throws manufacturers and marketers into a panic. And just as they have restocked the shelves floor-to-ceiling with the latest fad it disappears. The manufacturer's nightmare: too few at the start and height of the fad; too many at the end.

Fads are very popular in business. Shapiro (1996) defined *fad surfing* thus: 'The practice of riding the crest of the latest management panacea and then paddling out again just in time to ride the next one; always absorbing for managers and lucrative for consultants; frequently disastrous for organisations' (pxiii). She argues that the business world is full of 'breakthroughs' to achieve 'world-class' results. Just delayer or empower, change your culture while staying close to your customer; while having a vision and continually learning, then all would be well. 'The hard truth is that there are no panaceas. What is new is the sheer number of techniques, some new and some newly repackaged versions of older methods, that are now positioned as panaceas. What is not new is the need for the courage to manage: to assess situations, set an overall course or focus, think through options, develop plans, take action, modify plans, learn and go forward. In my view, in the age of instant answers, this courage is more valuable than ever' (pxvii).

Some fads mentioned are:

- *Fads in planning.* One of the fashionable ideas is *strategic alliance*, which means that companies cooperate, as in forming a joint venture, often across national boundaries. Airlines, telecommunications companies and car manufacturers do this.

- *Fads in organising.* Corporate culture refers to the values and beliefs shared by employees and the general patterns of their behaviour. Some believe that if this is planned, designed and controlled correctly, all the ills of the organisation will be solved.

- *Fads in staffing.* Organisations have to be staffed by people who are not only competent but also healthy. This requires *wellness* or *fitness* programmes and the management of stress.

- *Paying for performance.* Paying for performance is also currently fashionable. This means measuring the contributions of individuals and rewarding them accordingly, although the problems of measuring performances are often overlooked. Another current popular idea is *demassing*, or down- or right-sizing, which is a euphemism for laying off employees or demoting managers, usually middle managers.

■ *Fads in leading.* An *intrepreneur* is a person who acts like an entrepreneur but does so within the organisational environment. Intrepreneurs have been described as 'those who take hands-on responsibility for creating innovation of any kind within an organisation'. Organisations are meant to chase and foster these people.

■ *Fads in controlling. Quality circles,* widely used in Japan, are seen as a way of improving quality and making US products more competitive. These have been set up all over the place.

Fads have a life history (Furnham, 2001). The natural history of a management fad usually follows seven stages:

1. *Academic discovery:* Many faddish ideas can be traced to the stuffy and unfaddish world of academia. A modest discovery may result in an academic's paper that shows the causal link between two factors relevant to work situations. These papers are not only dry and complicated but also cautious. Academics underline the complexity of all the actual and possible factors involved. Few are interested in immediate applications. Their job is to understand, and definitely not change, the world.

2. *Description of the study:* This process can last a long time and usually involves a lot of elaboration and distortion. Someone reads the paper and provides a summary which probably leaves out the complexities. Often, the discovery is mentioned in a high-powered presentation. Others hear it and repeat it, each time simplifying it. With every repetition, the findings become stronger and the complexity weaker. Selective memory ensures that the crucial findings are recorded and embellished. At this stage it is unlikely that the researcher would recognise the findings as his or her own. It is the first step on the road to a fad.

3. *Popularisation is a best-seller:* The next stage is usually the big one. A business writer or guru hears about the finding and gives it a catchy title. One single, simple idea becomes a book. Indeed, that is why business books are so easy to read and précis: there is really very little in them. The average manager reads a few reviews of the book and may even go so far as to buy it. He or she is envious of the seemingly powerful results that occur when the technique is followed. It is at this stage that the fad becomes a buzzword and something all managers feel they should both know about and implement.

4. *Consultant hype and universalisation:* It is not the academic or the
    author who powers the fad but an array of management consultants
    trying to look as if they are on the cutting edge of management theory.
    Because the concepts are easy to understand and said to have wide
    application, the consultants seek to apply them everywhere, at some
    cost of course. The word on the discovery spreads like wildfire. Soon
    it seems everyone has to be empowered, reengineered or 360ed,
    everyone needs emotional intelligence training. Those who do not
    climb aboard are made to feel like fuddy-duddies and, in the words of
    Dilbert, doomed.

5. *Total commitment by true believers:* At this point, the evangelists
    move from the consultants to the managers. For a small number of
    companies, the technique seems to have brought quick, massive ben-
    efits. They become willing product champions. No one dares be scep-
    tical and challenge the 'evidence of success'. With hindsight it is
    sometimes difficult to explain why the technique should have had
    such an impact. Psychologists often explain it in terms of the
    'Hawthorne effect' – whereby workers boost their performance when
    attention is paid to them – or the placebo effect. They also sometimes
    talk of 'spontaneous remission', meaning things get better of their
    own accord. In fact, years after the fad has passed there are little out-
    stations of believers who keep the faith.

6. *Doubt, scepticism, cynicism and defection:* After years of heavy
    product selling, the appetite for the fad diminishes. The market
    becomes saturated. 'New and improved' versions are introduced. But
    the enthusiasm is gone. Then the mudslide begins. There is manage-
    rial doubt, then academic scepticism, followed by journalistic cyni-
    cism and consultant defection. The process starts with people
    pointing out the poor cost–benefit consequences of introducing the
    fad. Or it may occur because someone goes back to the original find-
    ing and discovers the yawning gap between what was initially
    demonstrated and what is now done. Then management journalists
    smell blood. It is easy to find disaffected, disbelieving managers
    happy to squeal. They point to the hundreds of thousands spent for
    little reward. The consultants who were eager to pick up the fad are
    the first to drop it. What once gave them credibility now makes them
    look like con-artists. They move on smartly.

7. *New discoveries:* The end of one fad is an ideal time for trainers, writ-ers and consultants to spot a gap in the market. They know there is an unslakable thirst for magic solutions. The really clever people begin to sense when the previous fad is reaching the end of its natural life, so they have just enough time to write their best sellers to catch the market at the beginning.

How long does the typical fad last? It depends on the zeitgeist; on whether there is a bull or a bear market and on the entrepreneurial hunger of authors and consultants. But what is clear is that there are as many middle-aged fashion victims as there are young ones.

Concentrating almost exclusively on higher education Burnbaum (2001) also looks at the life cycle of a fad from early enthusiasm, wide-spread dissemination, subsequent disappointment and eventual decline. His model has five stages: *Creation* with an idea supported by advo-cates/consultants who provide dramatic unverified narratives. The sample technique offers extraordinary outcomes. It is both necessary and sufficient to transform the whole organisation/sector. *Narrative evolution* where 'sto-ries' grow in every sense. A few counter-narratives are rejected and labelled apologetic, conservative, wasteful and self-interested. *Time lag* where fad adopters begin to evaluate the fad more independently and objectively. Acceptance of the fad peaks and cautionary stories arise. *Narrative devo-lution* occurs with increasing reports of failure and dissatisfaction. Disin-terested reviews report original claims were overstated and progress either never achieved or sustained. *Resolution of dissonance* of the failure of the fad: lack of leadership, intransigence of the followers, improper imple-mentation or lack of resources. Some keep the faith by blaming others which allows for the idea behind the fad to be relabelled for future use.

Bacal and Associates' website lists 10 fads:

- One-Minute Management

- Total Quality Management

- Learning Organisations

- Peak Performance

- Excellence

- Chaos

- MBO

- Matrix Management

- Team-Based Management

- Process Reengineering

They suggest that faddish management techniques do have substance and often have the potential to improve organisations. They argue that fads have a positive side: they provoke thought and discussion; they do produce change causing organisations to question their existing approach; they energise managers by providing a sense of excitement; and they popularise management ideas.

On the negative side, however, they waste vast amounts of time and money and cause cynicism. Indeed, a failed implementation of a fad can result in making future improvements more difficult. They can often backfire. If the rhetoric of the fad does not ring with reality there can only be problems ahead.

They offer six pieces of advice to prevent one being a victim of a well-publicised, but in effect, misleading fad:

1. Be sure you fully understand the technique before proceeding.

2. Fads are tools: managers need to fully understand why they are using them and how they can measure their outcomes.

3. It is easy to create the appearance of change and a sense of activity. It's harder to make sure the change is both real and beneficial.

4. Stick with the fad: steer a steady course. Don't be put off by initial failure or resistance. It takes time for processes and procedures to bed down.

5. Be prepared to put in considerable effort to evaluate/measure the effects/outcomes of the fad. Most individual measures are flawed but having a number of different types of measures surely gives a good sense of what is going on.

6. Don't regret a fad because it's old hat; too popular. Look at the substance of the idea not the fashion.

Fallacies in management

Fallacy is about deceit and deception; it's about guile and trickery. It is, according to the dictionary, an argument failing to satisfy the conditions of valid inference.

Alas there is very little evidence-based management about. Even MBAs are not trained in the scientific method. Hence they are often unable to appraise the claims of pseudo-scientists. There is a great deal of nonsense about from astrology to Zen. Managers, like the rest of us, are soon vulnerable to the tricks of the trade of less than scientific experts.

Marks and Kammann (1980) have sceptically analysed claims about ESP, precognition, clairvoyance, telepathy, psychokenesis and other related phenomena. They conclude their book with an appendix called 'modes for rationales or the art of doubt':

■ *If-what-then-what* – make the theorists be specific by asking what the theory predicts.

■ *Disprovability* – ask the theorist what piece of evidence would be required to disprove his/her theory.

■ *Burden of proof* – it is for the theorist to prove or substantiate his/her belief in the theory rather than your disbelief.

■ *Alternative thinking* – it is possible that other phenomena (mediating variables) explain the theorist's evidence just as well as the phenomena he or she cites.

■ *Missing negative cases* – very often negative cases (those that 'disprove' a theory) are omitted, so making the data look stronger. These need to be sought out.

■ *Personal observation* – subjective validations are not sufficient unless accompanied by detailed recorded observations.

■ *Testimonials* – personal experience is poor evidence because often people are not fully aware of forces acting upon them or their real needs and motives.

■ *Sources* – it is worth examining the credibility of a theory – where it is published, debated, and so forth, as these sources are frequently dubious.

■ *Emotional commitment* – the more a person is ego-involved in a theory the less rationally and sceptically it may be assessed.

■ *Ad hominen technique* – 'First a believer may hold certain authorities to be infallible, and quote their opinions as evidence. Second, he may try to place contrary believers into a category of bad people and thus reject their arguments out of hand. Third, he may turn against you, accusing you of bad motives or stupidity. All of these arguments are fallacious, and it is not only important to recognise them, but also not to use them. The object is to learn, not to win' (Marks and Kammann, 1980: 226).

Beware the oversmooth, overconfident consultant particularly those with a higher degree from a less well-known institution. Some learn the secrets of 'cold-reading' to persuade the manger of his/her insight and perspicacity. Over twenty-five years ago Hyman (1977) wrote a paper that tried to explain the tricks conmen of one sort or another use to persuade the naive client they know all about them. The article, which listed thirteen points (pp26–9), was aimed at palmists, graphologists and the like but is equally applicable to certain rather unscrupulous consultants. Think of the advice as given to one beginning as a management consultant. The thirteen points are:

1. *Remember that the key ingredient of a successful character reader is confidence*. If you look and act as if you believe in what you are doing, you will be able to sell even a bad reading to most of your subjects.
2. *Make creative use of the latest statistical abstracts, polls, and surveys*. This can provide you with a wealth of material about what various subclasses of our society believe, do, want, worry about, and so on. For example, if you can ascertain about a client such things as the part of the country he comes from, the size of the city he was brought up in, his parents' religion and vocations, his educational level and age, you are already in possession of information that should enable you to predict with high probability his voting preferences, his beliefs on many issues, and other traits.
3. *Set the stage for your reading*. Profess a modesty about your talents. Make no excessive claims. This catches your subject off guard. You are not chal-

lenging him to a battle of wits. You can read his character, whether or not he cares to believe you is his concern.

4. *Gain his cooperation in advance.* Emphasise that the success of the reading depends as much upon his sincere cooperation as upon your efforts. (After all, you imply, you already have a successful career at reading characters. You are not in trial – he is). State that due to difficulties of language and communication, you may not always convey the exact meaning you intend. In these cases he is to strive to reinterpret the message in terms of his own vocabulary and life.

5. *Use a gimmick, such as a crystal ball, tarot cards, or palm reading.* The use of palmistry, say, serves two important purposes. It lends an air of novelty to the reading; but more importantly, it serves as a cover for you to stall and to formulate your next statement. While you are trying to think of something to say next, you are apparently carefully studying a new wrinkle or line in the hand. Holding hands, in addition to any emotional thrills you may give or receive thereby, is another good way of detecting the reactions of the subject to what you are saying (the principle is the same as 'muscle reading').

6. *Have a list of stock phrases at the tip of your tongue.* Even if all you are doing is a cold reading, the liberal sprinkling of stock phrases among your regular reading will add body to the reading and will fill in time as you try to formulate more precise characterisations. You can use the statements in the preceding stock spiels as a start. Memorise a few of them before undertaking your initial ventures into character reading. Palmistry, tarot, and other fortune-telling manuals also are rich sources of good phrases.

7. *Keep your eyes open.* Also use your other senses. We have seen how to size up a client on the basis of clothing, jewellery, mannerisms and speech. Even a crude classification on such a basis can provide sufficient information for a good reading. Watch the impact of your statement upon the subject. Very quickly you will learn when you are 'hitting home' and when you are 'missing the boat'.

8. *Use the technique of 'fishing'.* This is simply a device for getting the subject to tell you about himself. Then you rephrase what he has told you in a coherent sketch and feed it back to him. One version of fishing is to phrase each statement in the form of a question. Then wait for the subject to reply (or react). If the reaction is positive then the reader turns the statement into a positive assertion. Often the subject will respond by answering the implied question; later he will tend to forget that he was the source of your information. By making your statements into questions you also force the subject to force through his memory to retrieve specific instances to fit your general statement.

9. *Learn to be a good listener.* During the course of a reading your client will be bursting to talk about incidents that are brought up. The good reader

allows the client to talk at will. On one occasion I observed a tealeaf reader. The client actually spent 75 per cent of the total time talking. Afterwards when I questioned the client about the reading she vehemently insisted that she had not uttered a single word during the course of the reading. The client praised the reader for having so astutely told her what in fact she herself had spoken.

Another value of listening is that most clients who seek the services of a reader actually want someone to listen to their problems. In addition many clients have already made up their minds about what choices they are going to make. They merely want support to carry out their decisions.

10. *Dramatise your reading*. Give back what little information you do have or pick up a little bit at a time. Make it seem more than it is. Build word pictures around each divulgence. Don't be afraid of hamming it up.

11. *Always give the impression that you know more than you are saying*. The successful reader, like the family doctor, always acts as if he knows much more. Once you persuade the client that you know one item of information about him that you could not possibly have obtained through normal channels, the client will automatically assume you know all. At this point he will typically open up and confide in you.

12. *Don't be afraid to flatter your subject every chance you get*. An occasional subject will protest such flatter, but will still cherish it. In such cases you can further flatter him by saying, 'You are always suspicious of people who flatter you. You just can't believe that someone will say well of you unless he is trying to achieve some ulterior goal.'

13. *Finally, remember the golden rule. Tell the client what he wants to hear.*

To help people think critically Levy (1998) offered 30 tools for budding thinkers. He aimed his work at psychologists but it is equally suitable for managers. Reading these and remembering them should help one be more critical of new management ideas and help evaluate them more accurately.

A: Conceptualising phenomena

■ *To describe is to prescribe*. The language in management is often evaluative as well as descriptive. Nearly every behaviour can be described in both positive and negative terms: 'frugal' versus 'penny-pinching', 'assertive' versus 'pushy', 'committed' versus 'obsessed'. The use of language is combined with value and perspective. Words used to describe the behaviour of self versus others, 'liked' versus 'disliked', are different. Descriptions take on an 'oughtness' an acceptable, indeed demanded, form of behaviour.

▪ *Abstract concepts are not real objects.* Just because one has a name for a process or phenomena such as renewal does not mean that it exits. Many concepts in management are not discovered but invented; not found but conceived. You can't touch morals or caress empowerment. So it is a good idea to think about management theories in terms of their utility rather than their accuracy.

▪ *We need and use multiple levels of description and analysis;* the level of the individual, the team, the plant or the multinational as a whole. Behaviour at work can be described at any level but we must not assume that the levels can cause each other. It is important to identify different levels of description and then select one for our particular purpose.

▪ *Naming something does not explain it.* Giving a behaviour pattern a name such as competency does not mean we explain it. There is a great deal of circular, tautological thinking in management. For instance: What is an extrovert? An extrovert is somebody who is sociable, outgoing, impulsive and likes variety. What is a sociable, outgoing person – they are extroverts. Many of the new discovered disorders in management, such as potential high flyers or creative genius, are nominal fallacies – they might (or might not) describe something but they do not explore its cause.

▪ *Quality and quantity are not the same.* Some things that we can study are easily classifiable into two distinct categories such as male/female; absent/present – they are qualitatively different. But most of the variables we describe in management are continuous variables: productive/unproductive; profit/loss. We often treat continuous variables as dichotomous variables: black versus white, mature versus immature. However, it is both artificial and inaccurate to group continuous variables into simple binary categories.

▪ *Phenomena can be explored by considering their opposites.* Often polar opposites (optimism versus pessimism; intelligence versus stupidity; profit versus loss; expansion versus contraction) depend on each other for their very conceptual existence. In fact without one, the other ceases to exist. Thus, when conceptualising a phenomena is it helpful to ask 'what is its opposite and what is not?'

■ *All phenomena are simultaneously similar to and different from each other.* It all depends on the criteria (dimensions) with which they are evaluated, with which they are compared and by which they are contrasted.

■ *There is always difference between what is and what ought to be.* It is very easy to confuse objective description with subjective value judgement. What is common or typical or 'normal' is not necessarily good. Statistical frequency has nothing to do with moral value.

■ *Beware one-size-fits-all personality descriptions.* It is too easy, but quite unhelpful, to make descriptive statements that provide distinctive information about a particular individual. These generalised statements are not wrong but, because they are so generic, universal and elastic, they are essentially useless statements about individuals and need to be modified by magnitude or degree to be useful.

B: Explaining phenomena

■ *Correlation does not prove causation.* 'Although a correlation enables us to make predictions from one variable to another, it does not provide an explanation as to why the events are associated. Further, it does not permit us to draw unequivocal conclusions as the source of direction of causes and effects' (Levy, 1998: 214).

■ *Relationships are as often bi-directional as they are uni-directional.* This means that we have causal loops, often called virtuous and vicious cycles. Factors may cause and affect each other. Thus unemployment may lead to mental illness (through idleness, lack of self-esteem, deprivation) but equally mental illness may lead to unemployment (because people do not want to employ the mentally ill). Hence one has a vicious cycle downwards whereby people become progressively less employable. Cause in one instance becomes effect in the other.

■ *Most behaviours have several causes and many determinants.* Productivity is not caused by a few crucial factors but often a combination of factors. The same is true of low morale: it is often caused by profound frustration, social rejection, low self-esteem and bad role models.

- *Not all causes are equal.* Causes of psychological phenomena vary in the degree to which they are responsible for producing the effect. It is likely that one cause is more influential than another. In this sense one could rank order the power of causes for any one psychological phenomenon.

- *Different causes can have the same effect.* Any observed psychological phenomenon might result from different causes. People may laugh at the same joke or cry in the same film for quite different reasons. Quite different reasons can lead a person to become a chronic absenter; a whistle-blower or a luddite with almost exactly the same manifestations.

C: Common misattributions

- *It is easy to underestimate the impact of external influence in behaviour.* People have a tendency to overestimate the impact of personality traits or dispositions on behaviour and to ignore or downplay environmental, social or situational factors. They see the personality, values and ability of individuals as the main cause, ignoring important social and environmental factors such as their manager or work setting. There are two reasons for this: cognitive bias and motivational bias. The first refers to thinking 'short cuts'. This means the observer focuses on the actor (the speaker) and attributes to success and failure purely as a function of him/her; the actor focuses on the situation (the audience) and this leads him/her to explain performance in terms of them (an appreciative, hostile audience). Motivational biases are simply aimed at making us feel better about ourselves – at falsifying reality and distorting the truth to make us come out looking healthy, happy and adapted.

- *Knowing the cure does not prove the cause.* This has been called the intervention–causation fallacy and what it means is that our ability to change, modify or rectify a problem does not of necessity prove its cause. Because drugs cure – or at least alleviate – the symptoms of depression, it does not mean that biological (neuro-chemical) factors cause depression. Aspirins help hangovers; lack of aspirins does not cause them. Factors that initially caused (turnover, accidents, customer disgruntlement) a problem may be quite unrelated to those that solve it.

- *The effect of behaviour does not prove intent.* We cannot determine others' intentions solely by the effects of their actions. There are many alternative paths to any behaviour in addition to the ones implied by immediate consequences. Why are people habitually late? They live a long way away; they do not have watches; they are disorganised; they are trying to punish those waiting for them; they estimate badly how long it takes to do things, and so forth.

- *How we feel about an event is not proof of its veracity.* There are for each group and each individual comfortable truths and comfortable lies; we also have painful truths and painful falsehoods. Our feelings are also not an accurate or trustworthy guide to the truth. Emotions are powerful factors in every observation or situation about yourself and others but poor barometers of the truth.

- *Extraordinary events do not require extraordinary causes.* Most people have occasional peculiar, unusual or lucky experiences. Often twins separated at birth, who have not seen each other for 50 years, have a range of things in common: they have similar habits, hobbies, preferences and problems. But so do any two adults picked out at random. Remember two children in the same family are on average as same/different from each other as pairs of children picked randomly from the same population. Very ordinary causes may produce very extraordinary effects.

D: Investigating phenomena

- *One can reason both deductively or inductively about problems.* Deductive reasoning is theory driven, top down: it is logic used to generate hypotheses but it is also prone to error. In general, we know salesmen are extroverted: Bill is a salesman therefore he is an extrovert. This is an example of flawed logic. Inductive reasoning is data driven, it is bottom up. Here we attempt to infer general laws and processes from specific and particular observations. However, it is all too easy and tempting to overgeneralise from unrepresentative, inadequate or biased data.

■ *Observing behaviour changes it.* When people know they are being observed at work they change their behaviour accordingly. This problem is ubiquitous in management. Job interviews, opinion polls, media comments are all particularly prone to this problem. To observe is to disturb. Hence the image of 'time-and-motion' experts who hide in cupboards so as not to let people know that they are being observed.

■ *Experience can create reality:* we produce what we expect to find. The self-fulfilling prophesy is well-known in management. It shows how a person's initial beliefs (prejudices) determine how he/she behaves towards others, which in turn determines how they behave in response, so conforming to the initial perception. Our own behaviour may inadvertently be shaped by others' expectations of us.

■ *We fit the data to our categories:* we assimilate to preferred schema. We categorise and taxonomise the world and develop schemas (categories) that help us organise our experience more effectively. Accommodation means modifying our schema to fit new information whereas assimilation (more common) means changing our perceptions and experience to fit into our pre-existing schema. Thus, prior beliefs, knowledge and experience can affect current experience, impressions and perceptions.

■ *Frequently we tend to seek information that confirms rather than refutes, prior beliefs and expectations.* We are biased collectors of evidence and hence should actively seek out evidence that could, in principle, refute preconceptions: that is, disprove our theories. To prove people are cooperative, we need to look for evidence of competition and non-cooperativeness.

■ *We stubbornly preserve and cling on to old, disconfirmed ideas.* The more we have invested in our theories and ideas the more we feel impelled to protect them. Hence, it is important to challenge pre-existing beliefs, theories, and ideas.

■ *'I-knew-it-all-along', hindsight is 20/20;* it creates the illusion of predictability. Prediction is difficult. We need to ask ourselves the simple question: how could we explain something had it turned out differently?

E: Other biases and fallacies

■ *The fits and myths of categorisation.* Does something fit into our management categories – is it by chance? We may not realise that a person or event is not representative of a particular category though it looks like it. We also may have motivational biases for things to fit a particular category even if they do not.

■ *The persuasive power of vivid memorable events.* How easily or quickly something comes to mind often leads us to overestimate its actual occurrence and frequency. Particularly dramatic events, graphic case studies and memorable personal testimonies in contrast to actual statistical data on occurrence (of, say, inner-city violence, recovery from cancer) are likely to exert a disproportionate impact on our judgements.

■ *We can solve problems that we can understand.* We often assume that insight is the sine qua non of success yet there is very little evidence for this proposition. Often it can be unproductive because it focuses on logical and rational factors rather than emotional ones.

■ *Every decision is a trade-off, particularly in business.* Every day we have to trade off time, quality and money usually settling for two of the three. That is, if things are done quickly and cheaply they are often of poor quality while if they are of excellent quality they take time and money.

Fashions in management

Thinking scientifically is a skill. Scepticism is healthy; cynicism is not. In order to be a discriminating 'purchaser' of management ideas we need to evaluate the evidence for them. Our inability to think critically will be all too quickly exploited by those eager to sell us a half-baked idea or process. It pays to learn the tricks of the trade from both sides: the tricks of the con artist and the criticisms of the scientists. Slowly we are acquiring evidence-based management science. It's difficult, expensive and often disappointing to try to prove a product or process works. But necessary.

Fashions are prevailing and short-lived customs. They represent the prevailing style in a particular period and could be said to characterise it.

Decade	Buzzword/fashion	Idea
1950s	Computerisation	Installing corporate mainframe computers
	Theory Z	Giving people more say in their work so that they will produce more
	Quantitative management	Running an organisation by the numbers
	Diversification	Countering ups and downs in the business cycle by buying other businesses
	Management by objectives	Setting managerial goals through negotiation
1960s	T-groups	Teaching managers interpersonal sensitivity by outing them in encounter seminars
	Centralisation/decentralisation	Letting headquarters make the decisions/letting middle managers make the decisions
	Matrix management	Assigning managers to different groups according to the task
	Conglomeration	Putting various types of businesses under a single corporate umbrella
	Managerial grid	Determining whether a manager's chief concern is people or production
1970s	Zero-based budgeting	Budgeting without reference to the previous years' numbers
	Experience curve	Generating profits by cutting prices, gaining market share and boosting efficiency
	Portfolio management	Ranking businesses as 'cash cows', 'stars' or 'dogs'
1980s	Theory Z	Adopting such techniques as quality circles and job enrichment
	Intrapreneuring	Encouraging mangers to create and control entrepreneurial projects within the corporation
	Demassing	Trimming the workforce and demoting mangers
	Restructuring	Getting rid of lines of business that aren't performing, often while taking on considerable debt
	Corporate culture	Defining an organisation's style in terms of its values, goals, rituals and heroes
	One-minute management	Balancing praise and criticism of workers in 60-second conferences
	Management by walking around	Leaving the office to visit work stations instead of relying on written reports for information
1990s	TQM manager (Total quality management)	Concentrating on producing high quality (no reject) products and services
	Reengineering	Restructuring the organisation from scratch, based on an understanding of function
	De-layering/'rightsizing'	Cutting out levels of middle management to produce flatter organisations
	Empowerment	Pushing down responsibility to lower levels in the organisation

Oscar Wilde said a fashion was that by which the fantastic momentarily becomes the universal. He also said that it is a form of ugliness so intolerable that it needs to be altered every six months. Indeed, the surest way to be out of fashion tomorrow is to be in the forefront of it today.

Furnham (1999) listed management fashions over the past fifty years as illustrated in the table on the previous page.

What is the current fashion? 360-degree feedback; training in emotional intelligence; psychological contracts and so on.

How are fads different from fashions? They appear to differ on three dimensions at least as regards management. First, fashions last longer than fads. Second, fads are often 'wackier', more unorthodox than fashions which are usually functional. Third, fashions tend less to be guru and consultant driven than fads; they are often responses to business necessity.

As customers change, so must organisations. Fashions may be responses to fads, but all managers would ideally be proactive rather than reactive. It's always better to be a leader than a follower. Just as there are fashion victims with respect to clothes so there are victims in management. Believing that bold statement, popular adoption and authorities claims is not enough to ensure that a fashion is useful or effective.

This book has short essays of between 800 and 2000 words that take a sceptical view of some management ideas and practices. As an organisational psychologist working in the real world, I meet the world of Dilbert daily. Dilbert is so funny because it is also so true. Incompetent, desperate or simply dim managers behave and do the oddest things in the hope of personal and organisational success.

The essays are hopefully light-hearted but with a serious message. They are designed to enlighten and inform. I certainly hope that they do.

ADRIAN FURNHAM
London

References

Bacal & Associates Business & Management Supersite (2002) *Management Fads – Things you should know.* //www.911.com/articles.mgmtfad.htm.

Burnbaum, R. (2000) The life cycle of academic management fads. *Journal of Higher Education*, **71**: 1–16.

Furnham, A. (1999) *The Psychology of Behaviour at Work*. Hove: Psychologist Press.

Furnham, A. (2001) Life story of a management fad. *Financial Times*, Oct 5th.

Hyman, R. (1977) Cold reading: How to convince strangers that you know all about them. *The Zetetic* **1**: 18–37.

Levy, D. (1998) *Tools for Critical Thinking*. Boston: Allyn & Bacon.

Marks, D. and Kammann, R. (1980) *The Psychology of the Psyche*. Buffalo, NY: Prometheus.

Shapiro, E. (1996) *Fad surfing in the boardroom*. Oxford: Capslon.

Accidents at work

The arrival of the 'ambulance-chasing', litigious American, accident-at-work television advertisements has focused sharply on safety in the work-place. If you have an accident *that was not your fault,* which is the crucial bit (said sotto voce), then maybe you have a (large, legitimate) claim against your employer. Slip on a wet toilet floor, get six months off and £10K compensation. You get the idea.

Lawyers will tell you how *few* of these claims succeed and also how *little* the average beneficiary is awarded. But this has not stopped hundreds of hopefuls pleading their case and enjoying the victimhood which comes with it.

But who is to blame for most accidents? That is, real, serious accidents such as the *Herald of Free Enterprise*. We make slips, errors, cock-ups and blunders every day. Slips of the pen and tongue and ordinary forgetfulness such as losing the keys are common errors. Serious accidents are comparatively rare.

The office, unlike the factory, the mine or the farm, is probably not as rich an environment for accidents. Industrial machinery, chemicals and simply the forces of nature are less likely to challenge the average 'salary man' pushing papers across the desk. Yet in every environment there lurks potential danger. The home kitchen, for instance, is one of the most dangerous places on earth according to accident figures.

Britain's licensing laws, only comparatively recently changed, were the result of restrictions brought about during the First World War. Serious accidents in munitions factories were attributed to workers getting drunk. Indeed, it was around this time that people began to talk of the 'accident-prone personality'. Such types have been variously portrayed as clumsy, dim or distracted. And there is something in the allegation. We probably all know someone who somehow manages without the aid of pills, booze or exhaustion to fall over, bump into things and break objects like nobody else.

Children have more accidents than adults, extraverts more than introverts, neurotic individuals more than stable types. But the quest for the accident-prone personality has been a little like that for the Holy Grail and the Yeti. It either doesn't exist or there are too few in numbers to study.

Cynics believe the accident-prone personality is a bogus construct thought up by insurance companies who do not want to pay compensation. Claims often boil down to *unsafe people* versus *unsafe equipment and systems.* Claimants favour the latter, insurance companies the former. Lawyers are happy to back either horse.

But disinterested accident researchers often find more faults in ergonomic and system design than in people. Study a major accident and the pattern looks like this: an equipment design failure puts excessive cognitive demands on the operator, who makes a series of errors, which in turn leads to a system failure, and then catastrophe.

Take simple items such as dials or displays which tell one how machinery is operating. These need to be visible, legible, intelligible and then follow habitual/customary stereotypes (for example clockwise versus anti-clockwise).

Usually it is a series of small system faults that leads to disaster. Essentially, system-based problems are caused by two sorts of issues: equipment and procedures. Accidents have been caused by equipment instructions not being written in the language of the operator. Select cheap foreign labour but make sure they can read the instructions. Accidents are caused because there is no way an operator knows whether doors are closed, tanks are full. Accidents occur because designers have sacrificed clarity for artistic flair. Accidents occur because vital equipment is not overhauled frequently enough.

But there are also all-important procedural issues. Observe the screen-watcher as airline bags go through x-ray. This is called a 'vigilance task' by psychologists. The operator really needs to concentrate. But the task is tedious. So the operators need to be rotated frequently: very frequently, perhaps every 20 minutes. And one individual needs to check the scan independently of another.

Because airline accidents cost so much in money and lives, ergonomists have been active in studying both flight equipment and procedures. Witness what goes on in a flight deck before take-off. It's a role model of how it should be done.

Accident investigators have to watch out for attribution errors: that is falsely attributing blame to a person, a piece of equipment or a procedural operation. Often it is a fatal combination of the three. You see the fault, dear Brutus, lies as much in our tools and our rules as in ourselves.

Acquiring people skills

Some jobs demand a lot of the newly trained. Not so much their job-related knowledge and skills but those soft skills related to that fashionable concept: emotional intelligence.

Young doctors have to tell patients that they are dying; young service staff have to face irate, assertive, bolshy customers; young priests and police-persons have to deal with an astonishing array of needy, demanding and distraught people. Young business consultants have to deal with world-weary, hard-bitten, business men twice their age; young diplomats have to charm, cajole and persuade a wide variety of foreigners often to act against their best interest.

So how to get the newly minted doctor or diplomat, policeman or priest, consultant or clinician up to speed? What soft skills are most needed? And how are they best taught?

Three weeks' intensive training might help, though all teachers know that 'distributed' (over time) are better than 'massed' (all grouped together) learning opportunities. Consider three quite different courses and the benefits they may bring: *acting*, *counselling* and *selling*.

Acting is about how to display affect; or emotion and much else besides. Skilful actors are adaptable and malleable. They can 'become different people' with different ideologies, mannerisms and emotional expressions. They can feign passion of all sorts, cry or rage on demand, and, they hope, remember an elaborate script. They know the power of the subtle and non-verbal cue and how to change timbre and tone of their voices to suit the message.

Acting teaches one to be acutely self-aware, rather than self-conscious. It teaches people how to maximise effect. How the medium, the message and the context together can have maximal impact. Actors have on occasion, and on screen, to be emotional and physically passionate with those they are not attracted to – but to look as if they are. They may be required to portray a person of a very different age, from a very different age, in very different circumstances from their own. Actors learn timing, dramatic effect and the power of the miniscule; micro expressions, barely audible sighs and gasps and how to work an audience. Useful skills. Our young colleagues need these skills: the skills to show interest and concern when barely felt; the skill to change the emotional tone of an interaction.

A second extremely practical course would be a *selling course*. All sorts of selling: cold calling, telephone sales, door-step sales, shop sales. And selling all products: duty-free and double glazing; insurance and insulation; houses and hamburgers; selling to people quite unlike themselves.

The attrition rate among certain sales groups is astonishing: 98 per cent over two years. That means only 2 per cent stay the course. Selling is hard. It requires social skills and ego strength; it requires persistence and ever-present optimism. It requires making one's luck. It involves learning how to hassle, negotiate and differentiate. Sales staff who under-perform give up too early; they get knocked back by their failures. They first blame the product, then the company, then themselves. They become depressed so that not even the thrill of the chase energises them.

What makes people good at sales? First, they need to 'read the customer right'. Customers have different, but a limited number, of needs and preferences. These may be deduced in part from their demography (age and stage), dress, accent and answers to questions. A good salesperson then has to adapt the sales patter to the particular customer: what features have to be emphasised and what downplayed; how to watch the customer's eye-gaze pattern; what sets a customer at ease and what scares him or her.

Sales people have to learn to play the long game; to be remorselessly upbeat and positive; to be innovative and adaptable. They need to have quick answers. And they should know how much of the truth to tell. Errors of omission are more shrewd than errors of commission. Sales skills can be taught. Some would-be-salespeople are more-or-less 'naturals', but all need to be polished to do the job well.

The third course should be a *counselling skills course*. A training programme that would equip participants to man the phones of the Samaritans or to talk to the survivors straight after a crash. Most people, demonstrably erroneously, think they are good listeners. A counselling course would establish whether that were true and, if not, how to become skilled in that area. Counselling teaches the power of silence; the power of touch; how not to be embarrassed by emotion. A good course should teach how to identify motives and emotions; and accept them; and respond to them. Good counsellors are perceptive and can, at times, be courageous. They need to know when to nudge and when to wait; when to give and when to withhold advice.

A young trainee, short on soft skills, could find job performance enhanced by these courses: acting teaches how to communicate, selling how to persuade, counselling how to listen.

Addicted to consultants/ consultant dependency

For a long time critics have argued that psychotherapy makes things worse not better. Psychotherapists, it is argued, diminish the dignity, autonomy and freedom of those that come for help. Therapy is a form of social control: it is an assault on the freedom of the individual (patient). It is a way of coercing people to believe according to the dictates of other people and to believe things about themselves and their experiences which quite simply are not true.

Thus therapy enslaves while it promises liberation. Psychotherapy, the radical critics assert, is a form of political control converting people's accurate appreciation of the oppressive features of society into the belief that their problems are caused by their own personal pathology. Then these wicked hypocrites persuade the individual to act in a more conformist and controlled, but less subversive way. Even worse, if that is possible, some therapists (deliberately) encourage dependency. Through a number of well-known processes such as transference, the therapists ensure their patients remain patients, unwilling or unable to make any decisions without consulting their therapists.

Occasional films that spoof the excesses of (American) psychotherapy portray the hopelessly dependent client unable to make the most mundane of decisions without a call or a quick lie-down on the couch. They are portrayed as gullible, rather pathetic victims of the psychotherapeutic process.

Now replace the word psychotherapist with management consultant. Does the analogy work? Is management consultancy a form of social control? Do consultants encourage dependency? Is there consultancy dependency analogous to drug dependency?

Management consultants are, of course, easy targets in the same way as therapists. Many resent their power and their fees. And the charlatans are more memorable but, it is hoped, less numerous than the genuine helpful professionals.

But there are serious cases of consultancy dependency. And the dependency occurs for many reasons. Consultants can make one feel important. They can bring unusual (and sometimes correct) insights to the business. They can act as crypto-therapists. They can do the dirty work of sacking and restructuring. They can tumble numbers and write slick reports. They can, in short, be a very helpful (if very expensive) 'friend' of management.

Charlatans encourage dependency by a number of processes. First, they usually promise more than they (or anyone) can deliver. They assure the helpless, hapless and hopeless manager that there is a silver bullet. Further, the solution is predictable and controllable. *All* one has to do is: sell off the manufacturing plant; or outsource accounting; or introduce training; or select for EQ ... or something and *all* will be well.

But the diagnostic process has to be shrouded in mystery. Just as crystal ball gazers know the secrets of 'cold-reading', so consultants learn the power of insight. These are: act confidently but also act modestly. Ask unusual questions but ensure client cooperation is essential to success. Be observant and a good listener. Flatter the clients and tell them what they want to hear. In a capricious and complex world many famous people – American presidents, British royalty, Russian tsars – have turned to fortune tellers for help. An air of quiet wisdom, of privileged insight, of perspicacious judgement is what both therapy patients and management clients want. They want to know there is a solution; that intractable problems are solvable.

Consultants can also be good messengers of bad news. Pusillanimous managers can hide behind consultants who recommend dismissal, downsizing or deregulation. Managers who get an expert second opinion to 'confirm' and deliver their 'tough' decisions may well find such help is needed time and again. Consultants can make their clients look good and feel good. They can do smart analyses which help in boardroom discussions; they can help with slick PowerPoint presentations; they can counsel people out of the organisation.

Managers who do not have the time or skill to collect and analyse data from their own organisation can be enthralled by the outputs of the smarter consultants. It is not difficult for consultants, like therapists, to make clients see the world as they do. They can easily come to believe things previously thought good were bad and vice versa. They can see and set up processes and mechanisms with powerful consequences. But they need their experts to verify these perceptions periodically.

Most managers have met others who seem unable to make a simple person-decision (hiring, firing, promoting) without first consulting their guru. They seem enslaved, not liberated, by contact with consultants. They are suffering consultant dependency.

Perhaps the Priory or the Betty Ford Clinic will admit this new form of patient.

Barnum in business

Phineas T. Barnum is remembered for many things. He was the super-salesman of his day. And perhaps the super-cynic. He is particularly remembered for phrases which capture his philosophy:

- 'Money is a terrible master but an excellent servant'
- 'There's a sucker born every minute'
- 'Every crown has a silver lining'
- 'Advertising is like learning – a little is a dangerous thing'

His story is a classic of rags to riches. He is a prototypic, nineteenth-century American entrepreneur who understood and exploited human behaviour. His eponymous fame has meant that there is a well-known effect in psychology which is readily exploited by business.

The Barnum Effect refers to the phenomenon whereby people accept personality feedback about themselves, whether it is universally valid or trivial, because it is supposedly derived from personality assessment procedures. In other words, people believe in astrology and graphology because they fall victim to the fallacy of personal validation; which means they accept the generalisations, the trite bogus descriptions which are true of nearly everybody, to be specifically true of themselves.

Fifty years ago an American psychologist called Stagner gave a group of personnel managers a well-established personality test. But instead of scoring it and giving them actual results, he gave each of them bogus feedback in the form of 13 statements derived from horoscopes, graphological analyses and so on. Each manager was then asked to read over the feedback (supposedly derived for him/herself from the 'scientific' test) and decide how accurate the assessment was by marking each sentence on a scale (a) amazingly accurate; (b) rather good; (c) about half and half; (d) more wrong than right; (e) almost entirely wrong. Over half felt their profile was an amazingly accurate description of them, while 40 per cent thought it was rather good. Almost none believed it to be very wrong.

'You prefer a certain amount of change and variety and become dissatisfied when hemmed in by restrictions and limitations' and 'While you have personality weaknesses, you are generally able to compensate for them' and, least accurate, 'Your sexual adjustment has presented problems for you' and 'Some of your aspirations tend to be pretty unrealistic', you see the importance of positive general feedback. People definitely, and not unnaturally, have a penchant for the positive. Many researchers have replicated this result. A French psychologist advertised his services as an astrologer in various newspapers and received hundreds of requests for his services. He replied to each letter by sending out mimeographed identical copies of a single, ambiguous, 'horoscope'. More than 200 clearly gullible clients actually wrote back praising his accuracy and perceptiveness. An Australian professor regularly asks his first-year students to write down in frank detail their dreams, or he might ask them to describe in detail what they see in a inkblot – the more mystical the task the better. A week later he gives them the 13 statements shown in the table for rating as before. Only after they have publicly declared their belief in the test are they encouraged to swap feedback. The humiliation of being so easily fooled is a powerful learning experience.

Research on the Barnum Effect has, however, shown that belief in this bogus feedback is influenced by a number of important factors, some to do with the client and consultant (personality, naivety, and so on) and some to do with the nature of the test and the feedback situation itself. Women are not more susceptible than men, though of course generally naive or gullible people are (tautologically!) more susceptible to this effect. However, the status or prestige of the consultant is only marginally important, which is of course good news for the more bogus people in this field.

However, some variables are crucial. One of the most important is perceived specificity of the information required. The more detailed the questions, the better – so you have to specify exactly time, date and place of birth to astrologers. In one study an American researcher gave all his subjects the same horoscope and found that those who were told that the interpretation was based on the year, month and day of birth judged it to be more accurate than those who were led to believe that it was based only on the year and month. Again and again studies show that after people receive general statements they think pertain just to them their faith in the procedure and in the diagnostician increases. A client's satisfaction is no measure of how well the diagnostician has differentiated him or her from others, but it is utterly dependent on the extent to which that client believes it is specific to him or herself.

The second factor belies the truth that we are all hungry for compliments but sceptical of criticism. That is, the feedback must be favourable. It need not be entirely, utterly positive but if it is by-and-large positive with the occasional mildly negative comment (that itself may be a compliment) people will believe it. This can easily be demonstrated by giving the well-used 13 statements with the opposite primarily negative meaning (that is, 'You do not pride yourself as an independent thinker and accept others' statements without satisfactory proof'). People do not readily accept the negative version even if it is seemingly specifically tailored to them. This confirms another principle in personality measurement – the 'Pollyanna Principle', which suggests that there is a universal human tendency to use or accept positive words or feedback more frequently, diversely and facilely than negative words and feedback. It has been shown that, according to the evaluation of two judges, there were five times as many favourable as unfavourable statements in highly acceptable interpretations and twice as many unfavourable statements in rarely accepted interpretations.

Hence the popularity of astrology and graphology; feedback is based on specific information (time and place of birth for astrology; slant and size of writing, correctness of letters, dotting of i's and crossing of t's, use of loops and so on in graphology. It is nearly always favourable. It is often the anxious (worried, depressed, insecure) who visit astrologers, graphologists, fortune tellers. They are particularly sensitive to objective positive information about themselves and the future. Therefore, the very type of feedback and the predisposition of clients make acceptance highly probable. Thus, if the general description seems true (and it probably is), people frequently conclude that it must be even more true when even more information is given. Furthermore, this process is enhanced over time for two reasons. Since Freud it has been known that people selectively remember more positive events about themselves than negative and are thus likely to remember more feedback that coincides with their own views of themselves than information that is less relevant or contradictory. Second, of course, people have to pay for the consultation. Perhaps one needs a wealth warning in every astrological statement!

Behalfers

It is probably the BBC obsession with balance that does most to encourage the 'behalfer': that self-appointed person who speaks on behalf of others. Whatever the issue is, fox-hunting or sex education; advertising to children or diagnosing yet another newly found behavioural syndrome; the BBC likes antiphonal chanting.

For every pro-lobby there must, it is decreed, be an anti-lobby. But how to find such people, who may not even exist? Fortunately for programme researchers, there always exist the media-hungry types, eager to hear themselves on the national airwaves berating 'powerful professionals' or 'fat cats of commerce'.

Behalfers claim to speak 'on behalf' of certain groups. Frequently the groups are, for one reason or another, not easily able to speak for themselves. So behalfers speak up for children, the poor, the handicapped, the dispersed or dispossessed people. But more and more they speak on behalf of consumers.

There are two fundamental problems with behalfers. The first is that they are nearly always unelected, except of course by themselves. They have chosen themselves as spokespersons, representatives or defenders of a group. Often they have not solicited the opinions of the group or checked their sentiment. Like African potentates who choose the 'President-for-life' option, they enjoy the limelight too much ever to check what 'their people want, think or believe'.

But worse than that, it is impossible to speak on behalf of whole groups, such as parents or commuters, because they are so varied.

This point is particularly noticeable when it comes to consumer groups. For a hundred years, marketing people have tried to understand the market for a single product, be it cameras or cars, shampoo or stomach remedies. Most have attempted a typological segmentation of the market force into distinct types.

These segmentation profiles have and can be done for the whole population or for specific products. Thus we have the following: from the most widely known psychographic segmentation system called VALS, we have nine groups including sustainers, belongers, emulators, achievers, experimentalists, and so on. Study after study has shown that people from these different consumer groups have different tastes and preferences for such varied products as imported wine, cold breakfast cereals, TV comedy, general sports magazines, fishing and visiting museums.

Even the purchasers of specific products can be carefully segmented, showing different motives, needs and purchasing habits. Thus four different types seek out prescription drugs: realists, authority seekers, sceptics and hypochondriacs, while all supermarkets know the difference between apathetic, demanding, quality, fastidious and convenience shoppers. Researchers have even taken highly specific goods such as quality cameras or cars and demonstrated how the self-concept and attitudes of customers differ according to brand.

It is therefore impossible to speak on behalf of parents. Notice that there are pressure groups who talk of 'pester power' and want to restrict, even ban, advertising to children. They argue with no evidence that advertisements cause (unnatural) wants which lead to pestering, which leads to purchasing. In fact the research suggests that parenting style and values, as well as peer groups, are by far the most powerful influences on children's wants.

But this does not stop self-appointed mind-guards speaking on behalf of all concerned parents. The simple fact is that they *cannot* or *do not* represent anyone but themselves. They do not even have good public opinion data, though they may claim they do.

Megalomaniacs with crypto-political agendas or concerned spokespeople for unrepresented social groups? There is no doubt that some behalfers genuinely believe they are acting in the public good. They see themselves as representatives of the repressed; David versus Goliath; the voice of the people against 'the system'; defenders of 'the right' against the wickedness of international capitalism (or socialism, or communism, or globalisation or whatever).

And they are profoundly wrong. Behalfers usually speak on behalf of themselves and nobody else.

The bullying boss

Is your boss essentially a bully and, if so, why? What can be done to change this behaviour? And are you to some extent the cause of it?

Many people complain that their boss is a bully no different from the thug in the playground. Bullying at work is any form of behaviour (verbal, written, physical) designed to coerce, frighten or threaten staff: either as individuals or in a group. Usually bullying is unprovoked, continuous and aggressive. It is essentially an abuse of power.

Bullying can be verbal (name-calling, teasing, malicious rumour-spreading), even physical (hitting, slapping, damaging belongings) but company rules, political correctness and threats of serious retribution have driven it underground. It is now almost always indirect: non-verbal, 'forgetful' (ignoring/not including others), implicative. Occasional arguments and disagreements are not bullying behaviour. Nor necessarily is raising one's voice an example of bullying.

Some workers report frequent bullying by their managers, even out of work. Senior managers are often the last to find out as bullying is easily disguised and well hidden. The senior managers underestimate or deny it. Further, bullied workers are often reluctant to report it. They fear retribution from the powerful bully who may ensure they get the sack, even worse.

But there is no denying the enduring effects of bullying on work performance. Bullied workers have lower self-confidence and self-esteem. Their concentration goes down and their absenteeism goes up. They produce less and are conspicuously unhappy.

Persistent victimised workers are socially isolated from the work group. They may originally be victimised because they are different: in terms of education, race, shape, track-record, career path, age, ability. And usually the work group collude with the 'bullying' manager. Bullies don't operate alone. Work teams assist, instigate and reinforce the bully by acts of omission and commission. Only a minority help the victim.

Bullying is complex, dynamic and widespread. Frequently, it is deeply embedded in the organisational culture despite the protestations of senior managers. The cause and manifestations of bullying need to be understood at four levels.

First, there are inevitably the bullies themselves. They are usually characterised by three things. The first is almost total lack of social skills. They can be passive-aggressive, or simply aggressive, but rarely assertive. They have almost no emotional intelligence and poor coping skills. The problem is this: they do not know how to charm, persuade, influence, so they resort to intimidation. They force others to obey their will by fear and threat because they can do no other.

However, the work group themselves play an important role in this. Studies have shown the existence of group attitudes – pro-victim or pro-bullying – which have a powerful influence on bullies. If the bullying boss is allowed to get away with it, it is almost always due to the work group. They stand by, silent witnesses.

The more the group are divided into informal cliques and gangs the more they are likely to ignore bullying of an out-group member, or even support it. Divide and conquer leads to bullying.

But the organisation as a whole may, in effect, be a culture for bullies to thrive. The real as opposed to espoused attitudes, beliefs and behaviours of the senior managers are important. Certainly official policies and practices on bullying, discipline and equal opportunities do play a part. However, what is official, often HR (human resources) generated, policy and what happens in reality are poles apart. The informal banter behind closed doors in the directors' meetings, or the men's room repartee, are better clues to the true nature of the organisation.

Finally, all organisations are embedded in the wider society. We have often seen media images of bullies, which may portray them as sad, mad or bad. Some cultures see them as inevitable, others as possible to eradicate. Public opinion can easily be mobilised over court cases where bullies are given either very light or very heavy punishments.

Few organisations have any sort of data on the topic: how often workers report being bullied; for how long; by whom; in what way; where and when. It is not clear how victims feel, or what actions they think are realistically appropriate to prevent it.

Some organisations see data-gathering as a dangerous waste of time. They believe a very small minority of 'supposed victims' are demanding ridiculous bureaucratic regulations because they don't like their manager who quite rightly tells them off periodically. Others see it as an imperative to understand and cope with the problem. They don't believe it is necessary to do good 'bullying audits' to provide the necessary evidence to legitimise the allocation of resources to deal with a problem which inevitably leads to reduced productivity.

The central question any organisation must answer is why bullying arises, if indeed it can be clearly and unequivocally established that it is. Is it due to poor selection of managers or supervisors? Is it due to them not being trained in the arts of influence and persuasion? Is it due to them being deeply frustrated by trying to fulfil unmeetable targets? Is it due to uncooperative, lazy staff? Is it due to the culture of the organisation? Diagnosis must precede cure.

Another crucial statistic is how widespread it is in the organisation. That is, is it confined to certain sections or related to particular demographic characteristics of individuals (age, sex, education)?

Certainly it is important that all levels are consulted in an organisation in order to develop guidelines specifying both what is meant by bullying and what should be done about it. Policies handed down from 'on high' are much less successful. Peer-led approaches can also help with 'buddying the bully', to use a current American expression. But one also needs to help those frustrated and unskilled managers who, for one reason or another, can't seem to motivate their staff.

Bullies are found as much in boardrooms as playgrounds. They make the life of their staff and peers a misery and they nearly always lead to reduced productivity. That fact alone should be enough to warrant doing something about it.

Business books and Stalinist Realism

Dictators throughout history have had an ambivalent relationship with artists. Architects, painters and sculptors have often been targeted as deeply undesirable citizens. Political potentates particularly dislike the 'avant-garde' artists and their fellow travellers. They see art as potentially corrupting and artists as having crypto-political, dangerous, left-wing agendas. Art is spin for the masses and needs to be controlled, indeed harnessed. Censorship is common in dictatorial regimes.

Fascists of all hues like heroic realism. Hitler, Mussolini and Stalin all took an active interest in art and the way it could be used to indoctrinate, even subdue, the masses. And curiously, despite their many differences, the dictators shared similar likes and dislikes in art.

They all approved of *Stalinist Realism*. What they approved of in this genre of art was that it was easily understood, simple and above all uplifting. So paintings and statues show handsome, brave, dedicated workers toiling for the good of all. Soldiers are fearless, defiant and self-sacrificial. Buildings have clear lines, are symmetrical and grand.

Art, the dictators believe, can be used to their own ends. It can carry important messages. It can inspire the people. It can enshrine the value of the state. It can communicate to all. And, therefore, it must be manipulated.

Could it be that the spirit of Stalinist Realism stalks the corridors of business book publishers? Potter around the business section of any bookshop, particularly those at airports, and you will soon see common themes.

To prove the point, try getting an avant-garde business book published. Business books, apparently, have to be utopian, explicit and opportunistic. Dystopian, subtle, pessimistic does not sell – or so the publishers lead one to believe. Dilbert is allowed, however, because it is humour: not real life.

The central message of all successful business books is that by following some common-sense formula all will be well. They do not dwell on the dark side of human nature – a favourite topic for artists. Employers are not 'polymorphous perverts', as Freud would have it. They are never depicted as capricious, irascible, or untrustworthy.

No. The Stalinist employee is of course a Stakhanovite: simple, naive, immensely hardworking. This person is loyal and self-sacrificing and prepared to give everything for the organisation. Curiously, the same is true of both managers and subordinates, trade unionists or not.

People are simple and so are processes and procedures that lead to success; or so the Stalinist Realist business books would suggest. Just put in place a certain managerial system or appraisal process and all will be well.

These books offer simple, somewhat deterministic, models like the profit–service chain that shows how one thing leads (logically) to another and that one can start (and control) a chain of events that will lead to ultimate success.

Business books can be frankly corny. Like Disney films or Enid Blyton, they have thinly disguised moral undertones. Good wins out over evil; but the strong inherit the earth.

Stalinist art is unsubtle and one-dimensional. It's not challenging or thought provoking. And it's never disturbing. The dictators often described the art they disliked as decadent. Business book publishers use different words but often have the same disdain for books that do not fit nicely into their preordained pattern. Does the market drive what sells? Surely. But has it been properly tested?

Stalinist realism eschews ambiguity. While most great art has, as one of its attractions, the possibility of multiple interpretations. Such a possibility is almost never present in heroic art or popular business books.

Business life, as we all know, is ambiguous, complex, paradoxical, ironic and downright bizarre. It's a theatre of the absurd much more than most other areas of life. But publishers rarely portray it that way. Hence the appeal of Dilbert and TV programmes such as *The Office* which show the truth.

Ultimately, Stalinist art and business books patronise and corrupt. They present a wholly one-sided, mostly false view of how things are. They are not in the business of understanding the human condition. Indeed the opposite. They are pure propaganda.

Cash rich, time poor

Your boss calls you in and makes you an offer. For reasons too problematic to explain you have the following option: a week's extra leave (5 working days) or £2000 cash (brown envelope, no questions asked!). You choose the week so he increases the money. How about £2,500? So if you take the money, he increases the time: 8 days.

This very simple question can prove surprisingly diagnostic. At the crudest level it tells you how much people are paid. Go around a room full of executives playing the game and you can get a very good indicator of 'who's who'. Sometimes senior people will hang out for over £5000 for a week's extra holiday. That's £1000 a day, but seems to have little impact on them. Others will take as little as £750, presumably because they need the money or love their job.

Cash rich, time poor (CRTP) is associated with age and stage. Middle-aged people have more money but feel they need more time. People who work in the public sector often need more money than those in the private. Americans, who may have only two weeks' holiday a year, certainly are time poor.

What does being CRTP do to people? The well-paid executive (say, north of £250,000), the shareholder-pressured CEO, the industrious management consultant: all have lots of demands on their time. So much so, they often experience price insensitivity. This may apply to big and small things. Shopping, at least for men, is more likely to be a chore than a pleasure.

The CRTP executive often whizzes around stores simply putting in baskets things that they fancy, need or think they need. They don't bother about the price or brand comparisons to maximise value.

Further, they may choose things that seem preposterously overpriced simply to save time. This is most often seen in their preferred means of transport: Concorde, the Lear jet and so on. They might be price insensitive but easily sold on time-saving products.

The CRTP manager is a fan of GAMI not DIY. 'Get a man in' is the response to both household and managerial problems. Do-it-yourself is a foreign concept. They are prepared to call in anybody who can help – now, and they mean now!

And this has led to the re-emergence of (effectively) servants. Of course they are not called that anymore, but there is a new class of servants whose job it is to give the CRTP manager more time. These personal assistants may do everything from walking the dog to serving food at dinner parties or even negotiating property deals. Their job is, in effect, to liberate the CRTP person from the chores they do not enjoy.

Because of this the skills of dealing with servants, lost for a generation, are being rediscovered. Personal assistants are called upon to do a bewildering range of tasks to liberate the CRTP manager to do 'what they need to do'.

The stressed CRTP manager needs to learn how to deal with servants but also how to delegate at work. Delegation takes confidence, perceptiveness and good judgement.

The CRTP dilemma has also generated a new concept: quality time. This is usually referred to as the time tired and listless executives spend with their children. The wonder and joy of a five year old wears off surprisingly quickly, so time-sensitive CRTP managers are often tempted to read the paper, watch the television or simply doze off soon after seeing their children or spouse. This is thought of as not good for either party.

Quality time means being fully engaged, attentive, disclosive, empathetic and the rest. It's hard if you are all 'peopled-out' and simply want to 'veg out' with a glass of claret and the paper. It's not uncommon for the CRTP manager to have marital problems: the spouse feels neglected, even spurned; the children rebellious and taciturn; even the servants might express job dissatisfaction.

Mrs Blair is a very typical CRTP person. Her job means she is surely cash rich; her family surely means she is time poor. She has to rely on others: to her great cost – not cash but reputation. It's a tough call – few deny that.

It's tough at the top: the rewards are high, but so are the costs. Time is indeed money. The question of course is whether the game is worth the candle. Remember few people on the deathbed ever said they wished they had spent more time at work.

Conference stress

For organisers and speakers, both the in-house and the public conference can be a source of considerable stress. Indeed, surveys show that the most common phobia is public speaking, which may affect up to a fifth of the population. Yet the need to give speeches to big and small, known and unknown, friendly and hostile audiences grows as a requirement with promotion to senior management.

Some people enjoy the showmanship of the big conferences. Marketing types and the odd HR specialist may even seek out conference speaking opportunities to polish up their am-dram skills. But, for many, the big, serious, open conference attended by competitors, the trade press and even the open press is a real nightmare.

The conference attendees may have to cough up around £400 to £500 a day plus VAT but, as organisers know, conferences cost a great deal to organise. Delegates come to expect the lights and music stage, which can cost £6,000 alone. The publicity, the helpers on the day, the special meal requirements can present real stress for organisers. As many as one in five may be cancelled because there are too few signups for a minimum payback at a crucial date before the big day.

In fact, with all the stress that is involved, planning a conference is not unlike planning a wedding. For the organisers there are half a dozen potential causes of stress.

- Performance anxiety: yes, even for chairpeople and meeters and greeters who want to look and sound their best to show off their company and its wares.
- Financial stress: trying to balance the books and having a 'great show' at minimum cost. The stress is even more problematic if conferences are supposed to make a profit.
- The long build-up for one day. It takes six to nine months to plan, advertise and secure a venue. For some, the countdown is like the ticking bomb in a James Bond movie.
- The management skills required: this involves coordinating suppliers, pandering to the whims of prima donnas such as the chairman (his wife), narcissistic speakers and so on. Organisers know they have only one chance of getting this right.

- Family disputes. Different parts of the organisation have their strong preferences about how things should be done. Just as at weddings, those with different religions have strong, often uncompromising, traditions.
- Fantasy to be realised: most people have attended the seriously impressive conference where everything went like clockwork and speakers, stage, and refreshments were perfect. It is often an impossible ideal to match.

So if it is stressful for the organisers, what about the speakers? Even those confident and accomplished speakers can get nervous about whether every PowerPoint slide has the company logo, indeed whether the presentation will work. Observe a slide-dependent presenter with the power off.

Many speakers are worried about the thin line between being seriously interesting and giving away company secrets. They seem less concerned about the line between advertorial propaganda and reality; or between frivolous amusement and information-giving. Perhaps some have learnt from previous conference feedback forms that jokes beat gravitas every day.

Some chairpersons get pretty stressed having to control egocentric, selfish speakers intent on doubling their allotted speaking time. Others get nervous about those ghastly moments when, after being invited, absolutely nobody asks a question. The speaker looks crestfallen, the audience uncomfortable, the chairman bewildered.

So next time you want to be enbadged, programmed and pre-conference coffeed, think of all the angst riding on the day.

Continuous assessment

At universities, just as in schools, there has been dramatic evidence of grade inflation. Nobody argues that young people are growing suddenly more intelligent or much more conscientious so the explanation must lie elsewhere. A favourite explanation is changes either in the difficulty of exams or the marking systems. Cynics believe both: standards are dropping to keep parents, children, teachers and, most importantly, the government happy.

Sceptics argue that this is unfair to two groups of people. Those people who, though not very old, went through the old system and received different grades which make them look less successful than their modern counterparts. The other group to lose out are the really bright people who appear to get marks very similar to those of their less talented colleagues.

But there are other explanations for grade inflation. One is very relevant to the world of work. It has been noticed that the balance between testing by examination and continuous assessment (CA) has changed. Teachers have given in to the clamour from students everywhere to have fewer exams and more CA. Students know that they often do better at CA: marks are higher, stress less. And so we get grade inflation.

But which assessment method is better? Is performance measurement in the world of work more like an exam or CA? It partly depends on the job. Cooks, actors and writers say that they are only as good as their last meal/play/book, implying continuous assessment but in exam format. Exams discriminate better: there is nearly always a wider range of marks. But are they fairer? Do they have better predictive validity, in the sense that they are more related to later measurable success? Despite the inevitable slide to CA, there are good reasons to believe that exams are a better form of assessment.

First, the ever-increasing problem of plagiarism is almost non-existent in exams. It is easy to see whose work it is. There are important factors of integrity in exams but CA opens the door wide for possible corruption.

Second, and related to the above, it is possible to argue that exams are fairer for the disadvantaged. Access to resources of all kinds (rich parents, computers, libraries) benefits students in CA and those with fewer resources have to struggle more to achieve similar grades. An exam is a more level playing field.

Third, exams teach one information storage and retrieval. Certainly, the advent of computers has rendered these skills less important, but it will always be advantageous to practice the skill of categorising and remembering information. Exams teach this skill in most disciplines.

Next, exams are good practice for life. Some anxious people may underperform in exams, but practice makes prefect. In the jargon of psychology, it's desensitisation for phobia. The more exams one writes, the better one learns to handle exam stress. In 'real life' people have to do things 'under exam conditions'. Making a presentation, solving a particular problem and having to spontaneously debate are skills nicely honed in the exam room. It is about drawing on a body of knowledge that has been well stored.

Exams tap both fluid and crystallised intelligence: that is problem-solving ability and factual knowledge. They measure planning ability and coping skills. And therefore they differentiate better between the more and less able.

In life there exist both CA and 'exams'. But the latter are better for differentiating the wheat from the chaff.

Control freak

One of the commonest accusations made by desperate and frustrated staff is to accuse a boss (or colleague) of being a control freak. What does it mean to be a control freak? Why are people like this? Can they be helped or changed? How can you best manage a control-freak boss?

The best place to start is to consider those things that are controllable and those that are not. We all know that the small print in insurance companies noting an 'Act of God' means an uncontrollable physical event. We can't control the weather, nor earthquakes, nor the sea.

But what about personal health? Dentists tell you that they can easily differentiate preventive versus restorative patients. The former believe they have control over their dental health. By brushing, flossing, a good diet and general oral hygiene they can control tooth decay. Further, with technical help and marvellous new whiteners they can, if they want (and can afford it) have beautiful teeth; a winning smile. Dental excellence and self-confidence are within one's control.

Restoratives are much less sure. They don't have a dentist and do not make regular visits; they only go when the pain drives them to the man who is famous for the epithet 'drill, fill and bill'. They don't go for three reasons: costs, anxiety and beliefs about control. They believe dental health is a function of chance: inheritance, childhood diet, the tap water, all of which are uncontrollable. Because they don't believe their dental health and attractiveness are within their power or pocket to control, they tend to be lackadaisical about personal hygiene. They are, in a sense, controlless freaks.

Dentists are eager to convert restoratives into preventives. It's better for business, better for the client. But they have equally significant problems with those who believe they can totally control their dental health. Dental control freaks refuse to believe that nothing can be done to achieve their particular desires. Something can be done, a lot can be done, but for genetic, historical and structural reasons, there are limits.

And so it is with wealth as much as health. There is a concept psychologists use called *locus of control*. It goes from extreme internal to extreme external. Those with an internal locus of control believe things are fully within their control. They are captains of their ship and masters of their fate. Their health, happiness and success are controllable and predictable. They can, they believe, have what they want because it is controllable. They tend to be optimists. And they tend to react very badly indeed when frustrated, when their beliefs are challenged or reality impinges on them. Such 'internals' believe they can have control, but they also *want* control. To be out of control is to be terrified. If you believe the world is orderly, predictable, just, and controllable, you do your damnedest to control it.

Control freaks believe things in business are perfectly controllable. They are made extremely anxious when those beliefs are threatened. They are just like phobics. They don't fear heights, the dark or needles, but they do fear being out of control. And to cope with this anxiety they try – all the time and everywhere – to control panic attacks by exercising control.

It is here that the most frustrating feature of the control freak is important: knowing how to control. We 'control' other people by charm, carrots and sticks, threats and punishments, incentives and rewards. Influencing people is a skill: it is a skill that salespeople learn. They know that people are neither totally controllable nor predictable but, with a decent cocktail of sensitivity and flexibility, one can go a long way toward influencing them.

The control freak is usually low on insight and charm and high on suspicion and mistrust. Control freaks are not people-people. They don't delegate or empower – why? Obviously because if they were to do so they would lose control. They tend to be frustrated absolutists: they want complete control but can't seem to get it. Under these conditions, control freaks can get very nasty indeed. They may spy on their staff and unjustly accuse them of manifold sins and wickednesses. They may explode with rage at being unable to get what they want. Or they may suddenly dump on people. That is why they are known to be such horrid beasts.

So the marks of the control freak are threefold: belief that things/ people are (totally) controllable; a morbid fear about being out-of-control; absence of skills to exercise what control they do have.

There is something worse: the controlless freak. These are your fatalists, who believe that luck, chance, fate, God, the IMF or Tony Blair controls everything and nothing can be done … save perhaps pray and await your fate. But, inevitably, they never make it to the top because they don't take action where necessary.

So how to manage the control freak boss? You have to work on three things: their beliefs, their anxieties and their skills. Start with the last: send them on an 'Influencing people' 'Negotiation skills' or 'Emotional intelligence' course. Create a safe environment to practice their new skills. Give them a very positive experience any time they delegate. Show them that control is not all or nothing. And that, paradoxically, they achieve more power by letting a bit go.

Delivering bad news

One of the more important, and certainly less desirable features of managers is that they often have to deliver bad news: the company is merging with a rival, finance is being out-sourced, a new ethnic and gender affirmative action policy is being or not being (depending on your view) implemented. The question is how to deliver the message such that it maximises the listener's attitude change.

There are two phases in this. The first is how to manage the meeting where the bad news is delivered. The pusillanimous boss from the conflict-avoidant company ducks out and sends the bad news via the intranet or personal email. The ultimate response is to deactivate the workers' electronic passes either to the building or on their personal computer. One learns one is 'surplus to requirements' the hard way.

Most organisations realise the way they deliver bad news and let people go is actually very important for their reputations but more important for those who remain behind. The non-sacked often experience 'survivor's guilt' and need gentle treatment.

There are two things bad-news messengers need to know. The first is how to *handle the meeting*. We know various features of the message are important:

1. *The quality of the arguments*. This often amounts to whether the speaker emphasises the legitimisation of the end good or the means to achieve it.
2. *The number of arguments*. This needs to be optimal rather than maximal. People can handle three to six good clear logical arguments. Too many and one overeggs the pudding.
3. *The apparent sensitivity and sincerity of the speaker*. This is the tough one and one of the most important. As all spin-doctors and politicians know, you must look caring, sharing and sincere even if you don't feel it!
4. *The reaction of others to the message*. People take their cues from others. If others weep they feel allowed and permitted to do so likewise. If others hiss, boo, shout, people feel being angry is OK. This is hard to manage unless one places emotional stooges in the audience.
5. *Dealing with questions*. People will ask many questions even if they are rhetorical. They will be affective – loaded with anger and anxiety.

They need to be dealt with openly and honestly – well sort of. And there will be a lot of them.

But the bad-news meeting is only the start. What therapists, researchers and counsellors know is that there is a predictable pattern to how people deal with dramatic changes.

The psychology of death, dying and divorce, like the psychology of migration and house moving is the process of adapting to change. What change-managers need to understand is the *adaptational curve.*

The idea is that when faced with the problem of having to adapt to changes people usually go through various stages. First they deny the issues; then they become angry; then they might try to bargain their way out of the problem; and then they might become seriously depressed. After all this, they may just accept the change required.

There are lots of 'models' of the change-stage process but they are much the same. What is important to realise is that many people do, quite naturally and normally, go through these processes. Their bosses need to accept this and help them move through the stages.

It is important not to try to push them onto the next stage if they are not ready. The speed of adaptation does vary from one individual to the next.

Being told you or others are going to be unexpectantly and suddenly made redundant can set off the process, however well the message is delivered. At first people are often confused and disorientated. They lose the plot. Some even express relief, gratitude and optimism. They seem uncertain how to feel and find it difficult to make any decisions.

The next stage is often reached very fast. It's simple and primitive: denial. People pretend nothing has happened; 'it's no big deal'. They try to minimise the impact of the change despite its being patently obvious to everyone that the change and adaptation to it is significant and important.

Following denial there is all the negative stuff: anger, resentment, resistance and the possibility of real revenge via sabotage, whistle-blowing and the like. Once these feelings are dissipated, the person often slips into the 'slough of despond'. Depression, discouragement and dependency are common – and normal.

The third stage can last some time but people need a hand to get out of it. They need to get into the idea of letting go the past; of leaving behind negative emotions. They hopefully begin to see light, the end at least of the adaptation process and the knowledge that they can cope with change, even enjoy and benefit from it. It's hard this stage, and various rituals can help, such as tearing up old organisational charts.

The fourth stage shows a return of energy and focus. People 'try out' their new role, status and organisational processes. Some push these to the limits. There is a renewed sense of optimism, creativity and work motivation.

The last stage shows that the person has accepted and integrated the change, and feels confident and even willing to help others adapt.

It is a simple, but useful and helpful, activity to show those in the midst of change the curve which helps normalise the process. They should be encouraged to specify where they believe they are on this curve. More importantly they should be asked what needs to happen to move them on to the next phase.

The process has the advantage of normalising the emotions that they are feeling as well as encouraging them to think of positive responses.

There are a lot of change consultants about. They know all too well that a combination of announcing the change inappropriately and denying the post-change emotions can easily cause the whole venture to fail.

Development plans

One way to ascertain both the age and the training experience of any middle-aged manager is to ask him or her what the opposite of 'strengths' are. If you think one has strengths and 'weaknesses', you are old-fashioned and clearly haven't been on a training course recently.

We have strengths and *development opportunities*; nobody has weaknesses any more. All non-strengths are areas of (potential) development. This naive, politically correct jargon suggests all abilities can be developed. Further it suggests, perhaps even more credulously, that organisations will provide individuals with some 'training opportunity' and that individuals will actually take this up to develop themselves.

This language has all the hallmarks of 'all must have prizes' and 'all things can be changed'. It implies that both personality and ability can be changed. The dim introvert can be developed into the bright extrovert; the neurotic tactician into the stable strategist; the pragmatic adaptor into the creative innovator; the shy technician into the assertive people-person, and so on.

The evidence alas suggests that personal change is slow, painful, expensive and difficult. It's rarely fun, fast and furious. But one is not allowed to say that. We all have to pretend that development is limitless. Swords can be beaten into plough shares; the blind shall see; the lame walk; the mediocre can perform with brilliance.

All this nonsense is the result of the self-esteem movement that argues that a positive outlook can and does lead to positive behaviour. The idea is that if you believe weaknesses can be changed, they can be. The self-esteem fraternity are deeply sensitive to the concept of the self-fulfilling prophesy. That is, if you believe you have specific weaknesses (poor at foreign languages, not good with numbers) your lack of self-confidence is perpetuating and self-fulfilling. You break this vicious cycle by the message of 'can do' and 'personal empowerment'.

But whether or not you believe developmental opportunities can be opportunistically developed, the question remains as to who makes these decisions. Lots of people don't want any development *thank you*. Development means change: that's harder as you get older and can be a long-term struggle. People need to want to develop before any development is likely to occur. As all trainers know, you can't change anybody against their will; they really need to want to change.

So who is the best judge of your personal strengths and developmental opportunities? Your boss? Trainers? Psychologists? Or just possibly you? Most organisations require, through the performance managements system, that an employee and his/her boss do an annual development plan. And they must do this whether or not the boss/appraiser knows his/her report well enough to understand that person's particular ability set or whether the appraiser wants development.

In most organisations the development plan is a simplistic meaningless ritual that nobody takes seriously. It keeps HR happy to fill out the forms and appraiser/appraisee happily conspire to do nothing of any consequence. One good reason to not take the whole thing seriously is because few organisations put any serious time and money into personal development.

The rich and the famous, and sometimes the indulgent or the desperate, choose a personal trainer. They know if they skilfully choose the right person and the right approach they can change.

Imagine the following assessment-centred task. The HR johnnies put their money where their mouth is. Your company will give you £5000 plus a month off work (not counting your holidays) as a real developmental opportunity. But you need to do a good plan: show insight into your 'areas for development', explain the budget, the rationale and the time. Clever ones will even consider how they or others could personally assess if, how and whether they have been successful in their self-development programme.

Some really think 'out of the box' and consider their development in the widest sense. Why not a spiritual retreat to teach humility? Or a white-water rafting expedition to teach courage? You could try a mini MBA at a posh business school or a mix of traditional training courses such as presentation skills, finance for the financial managers and project management.

It's an interesting assessment task. It gives assessment insight into what people think needs developing and how they believe it may be best done. It's about self-insight and learning style; about parsimony and waste; self-indulgence and self-discipline. And it's about honesty.

People, like countries, require substantial development. The question, as they found in Johannesburg, is how best to do it for real results.

Does coaching work?

The popularity of executive coaching has taken many by surprise. Clearly it has fulfilled some important need. Just as the rich and powerful once needed a personal therapist both as a trophy and as an adviser, so managers now appear to have the need for an executive coach and their very expensive conversation.

But what is the evidence that coaching works? Is there absence of evidence or evidence of absence? The answer appears to be that there is no good, scientific evidence that coaching does what it says it does – that is, deliver its impressive promises.

The question of course is how to answer the question. One clue may be in how scientists try to ask a very similar question, namely 'Does alternative medicine work?' Scientific evaluations have a 'gold standard' to evaluate the claims of the various specialities of alternative medicine. They call them RCTs: random, controlled trials. Better still, they are 'blind' trials.

There are essentially three features to this method, *all* of which are important to determine whether coaching works. The first is *randomisation*. This means that people (read patients or managers) are randomly consigned to different therapists, coaches or to the control group.

Why is randomisation important? The answer is that it controls for the volunteer effect. We know that all sorts of factors in the doctor–patient, coach–manager relationship can affect outcome. It may be the age, education or physical good looks of either party that affect outcome, rather than the process itself.

If coaching works should it work for all managers? And it should work for all (trained) coaches who follow the process. If it only works for certain types of people with certain coaches then we need to know why and whether some specific factor (other than the coaching process) is having an effect.

So a manager has to be (randomly) assigned to a coach. Neither party likes this much but that is too bad. We know that some psychologists have a selection interview to decide whether both parties feel they 'can do business with each other'. The scientific question is why the treatments only works for certain combinations of giver and receiver. If it does, this needs to be in the small (or indeed big) print.

The second feature of the scientific approach is the concept of a control group or indeed control groups. What this means is that some managers are allotted to a real management coach. Another group may be allotted to a physical coach or another manager. There are essentially two types of control groups: one in which the patient/manager does nothing at all and sees if the coaching experience is better than nothing. The other is where the manager does some other activity quite different from the coaching.

Control groups tell the evaluator whether changes in the managers' performance would have happened anyway naturally over time. It's called in the business 'spontaneous remission'. The body (perhaps the mind) heals itself. Nothing needs to be done for this to happen. Time heals. But it could be that what is having the beneficial effect is simply talking to someone else (about anything) or getting out of the office or being made to feel important. Control groups really tell us about the process itself.

The third component is called blinding: ideally double blinding. In medicine this means neither the doctor/nurse nor the patients know whether they are getting the (real) drug or a sugar pill. The reason is that patient and doctor knowledge powerfully influences the outcome via the placebo effect. With therapy you can't 'blind' the parties involved. However, you can blind the assessor, in the sense that the person does not know what treatment the patient/manager has had.

So after, say, six months of 'something' (executive coaching, exercise, nothing) the subordinates of the managers in the trial are required to rate them on their performance. Better still, some hard behavioural data are used to see which group changes most, and in what direction. Managers' self-reports maybe produced; but they may be completely delusional.

Does coaching work? Maybe. How do you know? First find, say, 100 managers. Send, randomly, 33 to a real manager coach; 33 to a PT instructor; and 33 to listening to music for a two-hour session every three weeks for six months. After this time, measure the managers' performance, self-esteem, satisfaction and the like. But best ask the managers' staff to measure the managers (upward measurement) without them knowing whether they were in the coaching, PT or music group.

If, and only if, the coached manager has statistically different and better evaluations than the other groups can we really say coaching works for everybody. If not, the questions of, for whom, when and how coaching works, if it can be demonstrated to work at all, will have only just begun.

Emotional labour

Even before the craze for emotional intelligence it was recognised that many workers were required to display certain emotions as part of the job. In effect this 'emotional labour' means hiding or suppressing real feelings while displaying other, even opposite emotions. They may have 'appropriate emotions' which they have to display more or less intently than would come naturally. Waiters and nurses, gardeners and fitness trainers, accountants and attorneys, psychotherapists and independent financial advisers all have to fake emotion: concern, interest, enthusiasm, and so on.

In many service jobs, workers have pretty little real feeling about their customers, either positive or negative. A customer at the bar, counter or table is just another customer waiting for a transaction.

Most service encounters are reasonably courteous and friendly. Those are the rules of social life and traditional etiquette. But the relationship is not equal: if the service provider does not like, respect or feel interested or amused by the customer, he or she can't or shouldn't show it. The customers can, however, reflect or 'leak' their true feelings.

The 'have a nice day' school of service demands that every encounter is the start, or manifestation of, a pseudo-relationship. Armed with customer information from a good database, the service provider can create an 'instant intimacy' based on professional knowledge. Even organisations as a whole encourage their customers to have a relationship with them. They want loyal customers who have 'warm and fuzzy' feelings about the organisation, the product and the providers.

But do customers want the emotionally labouring service provider? Are they even convinced by false displays of emotion? The boss might want the friendly service, but does the customer really care? Indeed is it not possible that the falsely intimate, overly attentive and disclosing service provider has a negative, boomerang effect? Too much emotional labour can be seriously off-putting. Some customers feel obliged to take part in the charade of friendship-formation and relationship-establishing service. The waiter introduces himself and gives a potted biography. The laws of reciprocal disclosure suggest customers do likewise. So both parties are engaged in emotional labour.

Some customers ignore all this false friendship nonsense. Others react badly with anger. But the judicious and perceptive emotional labourers should know how to present themselves. Almost by definition, good service is not formulaic. Emotional labourers need to be sensitive and flexible. They need to pick up the cues from their customers. What do they want/like/prefer from their service provider? Next, they need to be able to provide the level and style of service.

Consider how service staff are treated. Many are told to first identify themselves by name. Their voice, posture and demeanour should reflect friendly helpfulness. They are given the creed of the customer being king: the customer pays your salary. They must be flexible, adaptable, and helpful. They must 'delight' the customer. They must turn the customer into not just an advocate of the product but an apostle for the product and the company. And they must convert the shy, retiring as well as the assertive, demanding customers. And they must do this again and again – all day long.

Bob Geldof famously suffered from 'compassion fatigue'. One might easily forgive customer-facing staff who suffer from concern fatigue or helpfulness fatigue. The temptation to tell a customer with a starred first in assertiveness and a borderline fail in charm to 'bu**** off' is often overwhelming. You can push anyone too far. The straw that breaks the camel's back is a physical metaphor. The customer that breaks the server's psyche is a psychological one.

Physical labour is tiring; so is emotional labour; perhaps even more so. And it involves skill, tenacity and stability. Putting up with grumpy, unreasonable, demanding customers can take it out of anybody. Being remorselessly upbeat, attentive and caring can ruin a private life.

Emotional labourers often have to bottle up their true feelings until after work. This is not good for the work–life balance, as residues of tiredness, moodiness and frustration can be manifest at home. It's no accident that emotional labourers enjoy the gym. Physical labour seems so relaxing as an alternative to emotional labour.

Expectations ... and how to manage them

There are lots of books listing brilliant interview questions and answers. In an escalatory game of bluff and counter-bluff, both interviewers and interviewees buy these books to improve their techniques.

What is most striking in these books is that the questions and answers suggested are much more about impression management than really giving or getting information. The 'tough' questioner supposedly asks the killer question, but the 'shrewd' candidate has already anticipated it and has a clever, possibly evasive answer.

The selection interview is supposed to be about obtaining information to help make better decisions, choose the good, reject the bad. It is in an interview that both parties can get a 'good look' at each other and try to decide if there is a suitable match.

The selection interview may be the last time and indeed an ideal time for both parties to clarify a few pretty salient expectations. Expectations that are not really in either the job description or the contract. The areas rarely dealt with are things like *promotion*. When and why are people promoted or not promoted? Is promotion mainly based on experience (that is, time served) or proven ability? Who makes the promotion decision and what data are utilised? How long, on average, does someone stay in the current job before being promoted?

Related to promotion are issues about *change in pay and other benefits*. Will the salary rise in line with inflation? Who can expect a bonus and why? Does the company support people who go into part-time further education? What is the company policy on maternity and paternity leave? Is there an affirmative action policy? How does this affect both competent and able members from majority and minority groups.

Staff have expectations about *training*. Will the company sponsor a (very expensive) MBA programme? Will they allow time off for private study? Do they provide in-house training, offering useful skills that can be used in other contexts, such as interpersonal skills, advanced computing, negotiation skills?

A big issue is *flexitime* and its close relations; work–life balance; working-at-home; job-sharing. What are company policies and issues on this front? And, more importantly, is there a difference between the politically correct, caring and sharing talk and the actual reality of what goes on? The life stage of employees often dictates their preferred trade-off between time and money, status versus autonomy, but the balance should be discussed.

When do staff learn about company policies on absenteeism, lateness or theft? Yes, they may very well be given a wordy, noble and HR-correct booklet, but who reads them? Far worse it soon becomes apparent to any employee that what is written in the book and how managers behave are two quite different things.

If organisations conduct climate surveys, the results show that employees tend to complain about three things: pay, communication and morale. They believe they are, comparative to market forces, underpaid; that managers don't communicate honestly or accurately or frequently enough; and that morale (except in their section) is at rock bottom. Usually they don't have data on comparative pay, don't know what they want to know from their managers, and are simply wrong about morale.

Managers have a few, but crucial, tasks. They need to set clear goals, support their staff and give them timely and helpful feedback. They also need to manage expectations throughout their careers, preventing them getting sour, disappointed, angry and bewildered.

Yet it is commonplace that candidates who overemphasise their interest in pay and conditions, perks, holiday allowance, and so on at interviews will be given pretty short shrift by the manager who wants the candidate to be interested in the job for its own sake. Such questions are risky even for the genuinely enthusiastic. It is a paradox – candidates are inhibited at interview, knowing if they want the job they must not ask some pretty fundamental questions which may be important to them.

Solution – when the job is offered, or the candidate reaches the 'If this job is offered, will you take it?' question, then is the time to broach some of the issues above and explore the organisation's policies. By that time, the organisation will be feeling highly positive towards the candidate and the 'pay and rations' questions will be much less of a threat.

Expensive experts/
the consultant, the trainer
and the facilitator

What is the essential difference between a human resource consultant and a management trainer? The answer is quite simple: between £500 and £1800 a day. So what is the difference between a trainer and a facilitator? Or between a moderator and presenter?

The world of management development and training abounds with numerous people sporting fancy titles. Some are am-dram types; others rather school mastery/marmy: others barely distinguishable from game-show hosts or American evangelists. Some are relatively 'cheap and cheerful' in their appearance, their equipment and even their invoices. Others charge like a wounded bull, in the clear belief that if clients pay a lot they believe they are getting value for money.

Most trainers would prefer to be called consultants: the latter have higher status, are often better educated and stay longer in the organisation. They are called in to deal with complex problems and may meet the CEO, vice president and directors. Trainers stay in the classroom, report to the training manager, who in turn reports to the chief of HR, who may or may not be on the board. But both the consultant and the trainer share certain tasks: both have to make presentations; both have to facilitate meetings; both have to influence, persuade and cajole.

What is essentially the difference between the skill of a presenter and a facilitator? What competencies and knowledge-base differentiate these two 'types'? Presentation skills involve three things: a knowledge of the content of the area (by far the most fundamental); an ability to develop clear, memorable teaching aids (PowerPoint, overheads, hand-outs); and all those up-front, on-stage skills of saying your lines well. You need ability to understand the material but the skill of presentation can be taught.

The trick of finding adaptable presenters is to (a) take away all their technology and (b) require them to do a spontaneous presentation. It's the old trick of testing debating skills: the speaker first delivers the prepared speech, but then is given only five minutes to prepare a second speech. It is a test of quick-wittedness and general as well as specialised knowledge. If people can't present without all the technology, it usually means they are more coordinators of people than presenters of material.

Most of us remember A.J.P. Taylor delivering direct-to-camera lectures on modern history. His performance was utterly compelling, despite the fact that he had no materials at all – no film clips, no slides, no interviews, not even notes. It wasn't even clear if he was wearing TV make-up. His knowledge and eloquent story-telling skills made him unique.

Facilitation, at its best, is about understanding the process of group interaction. It is the skill of 'working a crowd', of getting a party going, of interpretation. You need to be perceptive, quick and good at both establishing and changing the mood of the group. A major aim of all facilitation is to help people articulate what they as individuals and the group as a whole feel. Facilitators should be good observers and processors. They should also be able to control a group, stopping loud-mouthed attention seekers from hijacking the proceedings. They should be able to interpret for others.

What differentiates these groups in terms of knowledge of the business? Facilitators need not know too much about business. Trainers should, but are frequently very narrow in their focus. Consultants should have an understanding about business practices and issues. Unlike trainers and facilitators, who work mostly with individuals in small groups, consultants usually work at the level of large sections of the organisation. They come with different backgrounds and expertise, but should have experience and understanding of such things as organisational structure and process.

Consultants may have to train and facilitate, but that is not their primary role. They need to access and understand a lot of the data collected by the organisation on gearing, production, distribution, benefits and compensation, absenteeism, and so on. They frequently have to set up systems to measure and monitor that which is not measured and should be. Through this they model processes to try to understand how, when, why and where they need change.

Consultants nearly always need to be really numerate: a skill never required for facilitators and very rarely for trainers unless they are technical trainers. Consultants also need to know – through both theory and practice – models of change, as they are nearly always called in to put changes into place. They need to know what typically happens when changes occur and what 'levers' have what effect.

Beware the facilitator who wants to be known as a trainer or, even worse, a human resource consultant because of the title and the dosh. Changing a name means nothing. It's knowledge, skill and attitude that determine what they should be able to do – and be called.

Failing in business

The statistics on business failure, especially with respect to small businesses are depressing. In some sectors, like restaurants, more fail than succeed. And success is defined just as staying in business – sort of solvent – for a year or two.

Why do they fail? Can failure teach us about success? Probably, but under a number of specific circumstances. The most important is *not* to ask individual entrepreneurs why they fail (or indeed succeed). The reason is they are nearly all victims of what psychologists call the *fundamental attribution error*. It means explaining away failure as due to bad luck, wicked politicians, demanding customers, unreliable staff, greedy banks. Success, however, is attributed to personal motivation, talent and ability.

Consider frequent reasons given for business failure – and the truth. The first, and rarest, is that old insurance favourite, *Act of God*. Fire, flood and brimstone. This does happen but very rarely. We don't have serious earthquakes or tornados in Britain. And that is the point of insurance. You can and should insure against these rare events. Paradoxically some businesses have been saved by disaster. Hence the crimes associated with insurance fraud. It's usually cost effective, sometimes a legal requirement. Second, there is *recession*. But recall that statistics from America show that even during the great depression start-up business failure was less than 2 per cent. In the early 1980s it was less than half that. Well-run businesses can thrive in hard times.

Next is *fraud*. Another pretty rare event: less than 5 per cent: the psychopathic partner, the addicted accountant, the bent bookkeeper and the devious and dishonest director who defraud the business.

But the puzzle is why and how they get away with it for so long. Anyone who runs a business must understand the numbers. They show trends, patterns and allow one to see the effectiveness of campaigns, offers, and so on. The financially illiterate deserve to fail. This is not to say that hiring professional help is not a good thing. It is, however, important not to abdicate or abrogate power to them. You invite fraud and deceit by ignorance of finances.

A fourth reason is simple *neglect*: more common, perhaps than not. There may be many reasons associated with this cause. The first is the haste of owners to open up other branches or outlets before fully bedding down the business. Too many balls in the air. The second is the opposite.

The obsessional, possibly nervous manager who cannot or will not delegate any power or responsibility. And then the paranoid tyrant gets ill and nobody knows what to do or how to do it. Thirdly, managers sometimes lose the plot quite suddenly. The menopausal middle-aged manager may drop everything for a leggy blond half his age. Drugs, drink and sudden obsessions from collecting to gambling can lead the business owner to neglect the business which then fails.

A fourth, certainly more common cause, is *lack of* sufficient business *experience*. This is often because of enthusiasm of what are, essentially, amateurs. You need more than cooking skills to run a successful restaurant. Brilliant hairdressers need not necessarily successfully start and thrive in a salon. Authors probably make bad publishers. Businesses need to understand customers, suppliers, shareholders, accountants, tax specialists. Indeed, there is a good argument to be made that managers need to understand in general, rather than about a specific business. Hence the rise of the interim managers who can manage any business.

Another related reason that may account for over a quarter of business failure is unbalanced experience. This occurs when well-trained enthusiasts who know a lot about a little think they understand how the whole business works. Stories are legion about the optimistic salesmen who did not understand loss control; the clever engineer who did not believe in marketing; the savvy accountant who thought people were motivated exactly like him. The *idiot savant* approach to management is alas doomed to failure because business is just too complex.

Brilliance or extensive experience in one area is likely to bring about too much focus on that area and not enough in others. Enthusiasm, good intentions and a good grasp of one area of the business are just not enough. But the most common reason for business failure? It is certainly unlikely to be admitted to by the fired, bankrupt or simply depressed business people. It is managerial incompetence. Management is about setting sensible and attainable goals; it's about using scarce resources wisely to support these goals; it's about understanding the various stakeholders in the business; and motivating staff.

Being creative, bright, hard-working and driven helps but it is not enough. You have to understand the business, the competitors and the market, as well as have a grasp of the basic principles of accounting, even a little engineering. Alas business failure, dear Brutus, lies not in our stars, but in ourselves.

Fixers and inventors: semi and real creatives

There is a great deal of nonsense spoken and written about creativity, mostly by those in the business. The single greatest myth peddled by gurus, trainers and their fellow travellers is the 'prizes-for-everyone' idea that we *all* are creative.

With very few exceptions all human attributes are normally distributed in the famous bell curve. This applies equally to physical characteristics such as height, strength and shoe-size as it does to psychological characteristics such as personality, intelligence or creativity. And just as it is relatively pointless enrolling on a height or intelligence class so it is of little use to go to a creativity training class.

Granted one can be taught better posture, which can influence the appearance of height; and practice on intelligence tests can have a small but detectable effect on scores. But short people or even average-sized people cannot be trained to be tall. Nor can those 'a coupon-short-of-a-toaster' do nuclear physics. But people like to believe they are creative – and intelligent for that matter. Hence the spread of the completely untrue and unsustainable idea that we only use a tenth of our brains or that special environments liberate our somehow 'trapped creativity'. That is not to say that creativity courses are not fun. They have an air of playfulness about them. They attempt to persuade you that, despite considerable evidence to the contrary, you are nearly a creative genius. And because there are no 'right-or-wrong' answers in this world one never gets properly evaluated and the useful delusion between trainer and trainee can continue.

Most of us know genuinely creative people. But it is important to distinguish two types who are in effect quite different in their abilities and potential: fixers and inventors.

Every organisation needs its fixers in both senses of the words: those diplomatic, behind-the-scenes, operators who through stealth, charm, cajoling or even threat make things happen. They are more wily, shrewd and courageous than creative. But there are also those technical people who mend the unmendable, adapt things quite successfully to be used for something quite different and generally 'keep the lights on'.

Necessity is the mother of fixers. A fine example are the car mechanics of Cuba. Every 40 or 50 something year old cannot help but really enjoy the time-warp of Havana where cars of one's childhood chug around 40 years after Castro took power and 'stopped the clock'. It's more than mend-and-make-do. Bits and pieces simply wear out; oils cannot be imported. So the creative fixers have little option other than to be creative. The same spirit and ability can be seen all over the Third World where soft drink cans are sculptured into toys and ornaments; and where little goes to waste.

Traditionally fixers are good-with-their-hands, but they have to have the ideas in the first place. They really understand 'efficient and effective' and can often work out how to do things better with what they have. Fixers are practical realists. They are often surprisingly conventional. Paradoxically they can be seen by others as inflexible and change-averse mainly because they are interested in things working better not differently.

Inventors are very different animals. They don't so much as think outside the box: they throw it away. They are interested in doing things (very) differently. They don't solve problems: but they can cause them. Inventors are the real creatives. They are usually seen as difficult, low on charm, high on egocentricity, totally impractical, completely unrealistic. They are full of ideas but not interested in how to finance them or turn them into action.

It is known that really creative people have an unusual thinking pattern – one that can't be learnt. They report that they cannot inhibit or repress seemingly irrelevant information from reaching consciousness. But what inventors can do is see the relevance of interconnected ideas. It is from this bizarre and often uncomfortable process that really original ideas arise.

Creative inventors cannot *not* think this way. Indeed it often gets them into trouble. Certainly they are often at logger-heads with the status quo. Many have a reputation for being poorly organised, unreliable, irresponsible, callous and self-centred. They can also be fickle, egocentric and rather too laid back. But if they are bright, fairly technically competent *and* well managed they are very valuable indeed. It is the last but that is the really hard task. Organisations need to find and nurture these people who are self-confessedly odd. They do not advertise their creativity and often have a very patchy educational and employment record. They don't interview well and don't do skilful impression management. They can have poor references, or none at all, and often a reputation for being unmanageable. But never underestimate the potential of the real creative.

Most organisations need fixers and inventors. But don't assume they will like or respect each other. They share different values, lead different lifestyles, see problems in different ways. And no training course can change that.

Fudging the happy sheets

While the government's explicit mantra was 'education, education, education', some believe history has proved it to be more like 'evaluation, evaluation and evaluation'. Politicians appear very eager to set targets and expend time and money finding ways of measuring whether they have been achieved.

Teachers and lecturers now face the course evaluation, which is taken very seriously. In some institutions, the instructors are not even trusted to distribute and collect the evaluation sheets themselves. It has been argued that they actually destroy, alter or actually concoct spurious feedback forms to improve their evaluations. Other argue that pupils are less frank and honest when handing a form to their instructor and therefore it should be done by an anonymous third party.

Some teaching institutions put these summarised evaluations on the web. It is soon possible to know the best and the worst lecturers in every subject as well as across the organisation as a whole. The best are sought out; the worst humiliated.

Trainers in organisations have long been exposed to the demands of the 'happy sheet'. Training managers and clients have little to go on to measure training effectiveness. It is simply very difficult to measure 'actual performance' or even 'learning achieved' by a before-and-after examination, so they scour the happy sheets, attentive to every hand-scribbled note and every change in the figures. Consultants and trainers can be hired and fired on the basis of their happy sheet results – and they know it.

Politicians and provosts, vice chancellors and vice presidents now all want proof of teaching effectiveness, of target hitting, of ever increasing value for money. Moreover the evaluations have the spurious appearance of scientific validity. That one can show that Professor Brown is on the 69th percentile for 'well prepared and organised' but only the 14th for 'really made me think'. Equally there is poor old Professor Green, a clear genius but who remains doggedly on the 8th percentile for 'clear overheads' or 'useful notes'.

There is therefore a new industry in improving course evaluation. Indeed it is more sensible and certainly efficient to put effort into improving teaching evaluations without actually improving the teaching. Below are some recommendations and facts from research on this topic:

1. *Be male:* Students expect females to be more supportive and helpful and if they are not they get punished. All students seem to be more critical of females, particularly around issues of availability and course stimulation. It is easier if you are a man.

2. *Be well organised:* Start and end on time, have enough handouts, check that the overhead works. Students get very annoyed with 'forgetful, absent-minded professors'. They notice if you are well organised.

3. *Be a soft examiner:* Lenient grading is a powerful correlate of marks for teacher/trainer effectiveness. Naturally, the really talented feel hard done by, but there are relatively few of them. Further, you can always defend your generous grades as reflective of your teaching skill – after all the evaluations support your position!

4. *Have early evaluations:* Don't wait until the end of the course, particularly if you know the students will be tested. The weak ones will blame you for their inadequacies. Catch them early, before they think about any test of what they have learned. They mark you higher if they forget you mark them later.

5. *Personally give out your happy sheets:* Choose your best lecture with the most amusing of all your profundities and anecdotes, then dish out the happy sheets. It helps if this lecture has a bit of emotional slush and appeals to their heartstrings. A happy camper gives generously.

6. *'Explain' the purpose of the ratings:* Be confident, be funny, relaxed, positive. Point out that high scores keep your research going; your five small children alive; the whole department in jobs.

7. *Teach smaller, selective groups:* The smaller the group the more you can interact with individuals and charm them. They also tend to be more selective and selected. Beware the disorientated, disaffected and disturbed hiding in big groups.

8. *Mix and match:* Go for gimmicks. Use the media; use new technology. Have videos, CD Roms, celebrity interviews. The modern student isn't into 'chalk-and-talk'. They have been exposed to the joy of the web, and fast-moving images. The salience of a particularly emotion-triggering video to end the course is neither here-nor-there. Show the best on or just before an annual appraisal.

9. *Entertain:* Students like you to be enthusiastic, expressive and entertaining. In one celebrated study an actor gave the lecture in place of a distinguished professor. It had little content but it didn't matter. Entertainment is the key.

10. *Establish and fulfil expectations:* Don't let students do a pre-course evaluations/expectations appraisal. Do it informally: find out the reputation of the course and the teacher and deliver what they expect.
11. *Model and echo students' beliefs and agendas:* Ascertain, echo, promote and adopt their views, even if they are hypocritical, politically correct and utterly vacuous. They like you to be one of them and therefore identify with you.
12. *Admit talented students only:* Set a high criteria for admittance. Dim, second-raters have learned to blame the teacher for failure, brighter ones do not.
13. *Evaluate everyone:* In the teaching and training business there are always those who exclude themselves from evaluation on pretty bogus grounds. Insist everyone is included. This increases the distribution of the scores, particularly at the lower end so your score will improve relatively. Moreover, by insisting on a no-exceptions policy for evaluation, you can take the moral, politically correct position.

The moral is simple. You don't have to be a clever, caring, empathic or dedicated person to get good teacher evaluations. Curiously, being bright, setting high standards and refusing to pander to students can be punished by poor evaluations. If evaluations drive the system, spend more effort on influencing them.

How to choose consultants

The change programme has stalled; the company appears to be haemorrhaging the best talent; the M&A (merger and acquisition) threatens to fail; the voluntary severance is only being used by those you want to keep; a mean-and-lean newcomer is aggressively eating at your market share ... what to do?

The answer is obvious. Call in a consultant. But can these slick-suited, silver-tongued, supremely confident, often managerially inexperienced and overpaid young people really help solve the problem?

Just as everyone has a 'better-than-yours' flight-delay story, so they can tell a consultant-from-hell tale. But most can also, though with less humour, recall the case when a good management consultant really did make a difference. The question is, how to tell the difference? How to discriminate the good from bad?

For most in the game, two criteria are applied: reputation and price. They might phone up a friend, read an article in a business magazine, or recall a personal experience when consultants from ABC delivered what they promised. Reputation is a delicate plant: easily destroyed, difficult to nurture, and whose beauty is often in the eye of the beholder's personal taste. People can trade on a long past, undeserved reputation. And, through chance alone, people who deserve a good reputation might have had little opportunity to develop it and spread the word.

The second criterion is, of course, price. Some consultants' personal criteria for establishing their daily rate appears to be the ability to mention some (outrageous) number without smiling. Just as with all products and services, there is a pretty low correlation between quality and price. Expensive does not mean high quality; nor does cheap necessarily mean cheerful.

There have to be financial considerations in choosing a consultant, but they should be done after the best consultants have been selected.

There are a number of important criteria to apply to the selection process. Perhaps least important, but still worth considering, is the issue of *certification and experience*. What is the technical and general managerial knowledge base of the consultants? Are they up to date? Is it all theory and no practical experience, or all personal experience with no thinking?

Next, how good are their *explanations* for their processes? Can they explain clearly and without jargon, how the intervention works and 'where the wires go?' If it is full of platitudes and hot air, or you can't understand it, it is important to challenge its nonsense. They have to explain not what they plan to do, but why they are choosing to do it.

Third, you need evidence of their *evaluation studies*. This means, how have they, and do they plan to evaluate what they do? Do they have disinterested, impartial evidence that their strategy brings about the desired effects? What is the nature of the evidence? Is it anecdotal post-hoc rationalisation or are there numbers involved? Who does the evaluation and can they be trusted?

Fourth, one wants to know about the proposed *method* used. Why one rather than another? Why things in a particular order? What will these methods achieve and what are their particular drawbacks? The sorts of answers to these questions tell one quite quickly the quality of consultants.

The fifth criterion is perhaps the most interesting. Many clients correctly suspect that despite all the talk of uniqueness and tailoring approaches to particular and special needs (blah blah), consultants simply give one the standard, off-the-shelf answers/advice. So the trap to lure consultants into is that of *replication*. Question: how do they know the procedure will work? Answer: because it has worked in the past! But that means you are doing the same thing as you did in the past, and you promised us it would be unique!

Good consultants easily pass the five finger tests. They have the learning, can explain the process, volunteer to monitor their effectiveness, use proven methods and understand where things have really to be tailored and when not.

Once you know the answers to the questions, start haggling about price. You will be surprised how many smart, pompous, know-alls fall at the first hurdle. You won't even need to enquire about their preposterous daily rate.

Hypocritical management speak

Many captains of industry argue passionately even eloquently for the market economy. Market forces, they argue, do and should determine the price of products and labour. They also supposedly determine their generous salaries. It has become fashionable for what the tabloids call 'fat cats' to explain their 'appropriate packages' in terms of (global) market forces. 'It is the international going rate for the job. You can't get good people unless you pay competitive salaries.' And the latter are determined by market forces – well sort of! Most favour as little regulation as possible be it from London or Brussels, unless of course they are immediate beneficiaries of it. They see controls, regulations, tariffs and barriers as red tape: bad for themselves and bad for the consumer.

It is indeed almost impossible to find support for the planned and controlled model of the old Soviet Union. There one saw bureaucratic monopolies, where central planning determined the price of everything with seemingly little reference to consumer needs and wants. Pointless departments were subsidised. No one knew the real cost of things because market forces did not apply. Faceless Nyet-sayers held down safe jobs of little use to anyone. But the West won; at least on the macro-economic model. This is however, not true of the micro-economy of the average firm run, often, by those political philosophies of CEOs.

Imagine the big organisations run like the national economy with market forces operating. Each department (business unit) would be free to buy and sell its products wherever it wanted, free of regulation from corporate HQ. Human resources, the training department, corporate lawyers and other 'support staff' would swell or shrink to what the market wanted. If the internal people were cheap, efficient and competent they would be used; if not one would be free to go elsewhere.

Take training: this could be sold internally at a set price. Purchasers could be trained by internal or external people whichever was better value. Some organisations have done this, though people complain that there are no quality checks. And in some very advanced and ever courageous organisations each individual is given a personal training budget and the liberty to spend that money as he/she wishes, hopefully with some sort of reasonable justification.

The issue is this: how far should one go in either creating an internal market or letting market forces really operate in the business? Right-wing, liberal economists see the internal market as being the most efficient. Market forces bring the Darwinian scythe to ever growing weeds of bureaucracy. They encourage competition and as a result excellence.

But can and does this work in organisations? While it makes perfect sense to adapt that model when it comes to, say, marketing, how does one apply it to, say, human resources, strategic planning or health and safety? The brighter and more zealous will of course be able to find ways of introducing the free market to all aspects of the business.

But most managers are content to rob Peter to pay Paul and they are also able to turn a blind eye to within-business subsidisation while simultaneously calling for a free market between businesses.

A second related area in which 'big-chief' senior managers speak with 'forked tongue' is performance appraisal. There is a lot of talk about equitably based pay-for-performance systems based on a simple idea: there is a direct, clear, relationship between output and reward. Those whose effort and ability lead to best results get rewarded accordingly, equitably. It has been known since the 1920s that the most productive employee is about 2.5 times more productive than the least productive *doing the same job* (and with the same experience and training). It's a rule of thumb but with reasonable validity.

The question is, of course, is their productivity reflected in pay? And the answer, despite all that talk of equity, is a resounding – NO. The reasons for this situation are manifold: the power of unions to set pay scales for job irrespective of productivity; a history of service being rated as more important than productivity; a pusillanimous management who won't bite the bullet and give a few a lot and a lot nothing in performance-related pay.

Most people are unhappy with their appraisal systems. There are many reasons for that but perhaps the most common complaints are twofold. First, ratings are often unfair because of the different standards imposed by different managers. But more important is the self-evident and obvious gap between actual output differences and differential performance-related pay. That is, the highest rated gets a few hundred pounds more than the lowest. But if the principle of equity were really working, a few would get a great deal and quite a lot nothing at all.

So we find talk of equity, market forces, competition and the like dribbling out of the mouths of the captains of industry, whose personal bonuses do not seem closely related to their performance.

Ice breakers

All trainers like to start (adult) courses of all sorts with an ice breaker. They believe that participants need to be 'energised' by a bit of fun; perhaps some physical activity which lets them have a bit of non-verbal contact.

Traditionally, most courses (seminars, workshops, colloquia) begin in a standard manner. First the instructor (teacher, coach, seminar leader) introduces him/herself. The mixture of self-disclosure, aggrandisement and crypto-humility is well rehearsed. Trainers are, at once, trying to model what they want others to do, establish their credibility and warm up the class.

Next the instructor invites people to go round the table saying a few things about themselves, such as, their job titles, how many years they have worked for the company and perhaps a little something about their private lives. Anodyne ephemera follow. Most people are used to the process. Some get rather nervous about the whole thing.

After this little exercise, the ice-breaking activity may occur. There are books for trainers, listing recommended activities. They range from the bizarre to the daft, from 1960's California-airhead to quasi SAS commando training. They last anything from three to ten minutes and might even have a 'message attached'.

The format works well enough, but over the past few years, the American love of self-disclosure and psychotherapy has led to the development of a new sort of course-start technique. It is much more psychological than physical, though it can be both. The idea is really to get to know somebody quickly and well. Below are a few examples of the genre.

The lying game

Delegates and course attenders are invited to state three things about themselves but with a catch; two are to be true and one false. Their task is to both amuse and trick others by seeing if they can hoodwink them.

The game can work very well, particularly if a few outlandish extraverts begin with some hot items, usually about relationships, work successes and failures or childhood experiences.

The game is actually a real test of skills, because each person needs three skills: an ability to see themselves as others see them; an ability to 'read the audience'; and an ability to dissimulate convincingly. They can provide wonderful illustrations, if one is on a course, of interpersonal skills or even leadership.

And what emerges is truly interesting. Unless people are particularly guarded, they can reveal things about themselves perhaps few could easily guess. A great way to get the party going.

Deprivations

The task here is just as psychologically interesting though sometimes very difficult for candidates. Again one says three things about oneself. This time they are all true. What they present are facts about oneself which reveal what one *has not* done that others have done. The skills again is 'reading the audience' for their typical biography.

Thus you could say 'I have never seen Hamlet'. A bad start if the seminar is for trainee milkmen; but pretty good if they are merchant bankers. You win a point only if you honestly disclose a deprivation of which everyone else has experience. 'I have never been to Greece'; 'I have never had a performance appraisal'; 'I have never used a computer' are useful examples.

It's all very British because the losers are the winners: those who have been 'deprived' end up winning. Of course, and here is the rub, deprived has many meanings. And just as 'does not tolerate fools easily' is a code for 'very bright', so deprivations can in fact be indications of success: 'I have never had a filling'; 'I have never failed an exam in my life'; 'I have never had a day's work absence in the last decade'.

You can, if lucky, get a 'lot of stuff' from this little exercise.

Favourite compliments

This is much shorter but can be very revealing. The candidates are asked to imagine a person whom they know well, *and who knows them well*. They are told to imagine the person is being *totally honest*. The question they have to answer is what would be the nicest or favourite compliment from such a person? The key is the honesty and familiarity of the fantasy compliment-giver.

The theory, if it is that, behind this particular nugget of self-disclosure, is that favourite compliments belie both values and insecurities. Favourite compliments show people's real values – things of uttermost importance to themselves. They also show, however, things one does not really feel very confident about. Things one is sure are true are unlikely to be preferred, honestly meant compliments.

The trouble with the ice breaker is, what does the trainer say if someone says 'I like to be thought of as a great lover' or 'I would like to be a sincere friend'? The problem is that favourite compliments can be pretty humiliating.

Sincere one-to-one

Given anybody in the world, living or dead, past or present, with whom would you most like to have a really good chin-wag? Occasionally we all feel the need to discuss the meaning of life, the answers to the hard questions, and so on. So whom do we seek for wisdom, succour, comfort or guidance? This is another starter. Delegates nominate all kinds of odd people – dead parents, old teachers, the Saints, politicians and philosophers. They certainly represent a very odd collection if it is thought they are a repository of wisdom.

People can perform this task, though they struggle a bit with the follow-up question concerning what they want to talk about. Some answers can be wonderfully pretentious 'I would like to discuss the real meaning of dialectic materialism with Marx' or 'I would love to have a real one-to-one with Mother Theresa and discuss the importance of humility'.

There are other variations on these 'round-the-table' ice breakers. Some fail badly because people won't play the game. Others make people pretty defensive, which is exactly the opposite effect that they are intended to have. But the right game for the right group can really 'get the party going' even early on a Monday morning in the training department.

Integrity

What is the single most desirable characteristic employees want in their employer? Imagination, maturity, inspiration, fair-mindedness? No. How about loyalty, concern, support, dependability or competence? No.

The answer is honesty or integrity. A recent British study published in the *Journal of Managerial Psychology* (Furnham, 2003, **17**: 655) confirmed an earlier American study that showed that when asked to rate 20 positive things we might want in a manager, honesty comes out top. Integrity is about being incorruptible; about uncompromisingly adhering to a moral code; about being sound, complete and whole. It's about being trustworthy, telling the truth, facing up to responsibilities. It's about being consistent in the application of an ethical code. It is about those simple and forgotten rules of behaviour we learn in our schooldays.

But the cynics seem to suggest you can't really have integrity at work. Integrity, it is said, is a lofty attitude assumed by someone who is unemployed. And honesty is only what you will do or say if you have a guarantee that you will never be found out. Jerome K. Jerome recommended that one always tell the truth, unless one is a good liar. In the new world of spin honesty has taken on a rather slippery hue. This is not the world of good or bad, truth or lie, fact or fiction. There are, it seems, degrees of truth.

As Noel Coward observed, it's discouraging to think how many people are shocked by honesty and how few by deceit. Perhaps we have become so immune to bluff, bravado and, frankly, the bullshit of business that we have come to be surprised by frankness. Ever heard of the politician who sees by-election results as anything but positive or CEOs who attribute good profits to personal skill or strategy, but poor results to bear markets, and a general down-turn in the economy? Ever heard of students who assert that their failures are due to an unenviable mix of low ability and little effort, or their successes to the brilliance of their teachers?

Business, like politics, is about spin. You have to appear to be sincere whether you mean it or not. Sincerity and honesty are seen to be dangerous. Hence the need for media training for all executives. The facts need to be massaged, packaged and presented. PR is the activity of trying to persuade others of what you yourself might not even believe. The trouble is, that after a while, it becomes easy for managers to believe their own propaganda. Memory can play many tricks but seems to be, at least for most people, psychologically protective. So much so that the past seems much more in dispute than the future.

Alas, honesty, virtue and sincerity have never been as respectable as money. In business it is said, without the benefit of scruples your money soon quadruples. The main objection to honesty is the price – or is it? The problem and the benefit is truth. People begin to get reputations for honesty and integrity. But it is a frail plant and once lost takes ages to regain. People prefer the truth. Frustrated travellers all say they would rather be told exactly what the problem is than hear the flimflam, euphemisms and standard phrases that are dished out when things go wrong. At least they can make plans, contact others and rearrange their schedules.

All employees want managers whom they can trust. Try the 'good news – bad news' question. The vast majority of people want the bad news first. Yes, they want things presented tactfully, but realistically. They don't want half-truths, sanitised presentation, feel-good facts.

Churchill told people the truth: often to his personal detriment. The BBC also had the reputation for unbiased reporting. No flimflam, no spin, no porkies. There is a time and a way to tell the truth so people can hear it. And that is what they appreciate in their managers.

That said, it is far from certain that we have a case of the more the better. Can one have too much integrity? Can one be too ethical? Ethics, integrity and honesty are too slippery to be black/white, on/off, yes/no issues. There are degrees of sinning even in the Catholic Church. But can one be too saintly?

The answer seems to be yes. The zealot and the bigot can be people with too much integrity. Integrity with a fundamentalist flavour can be pretty frightening. Scripture, the law and ethical codes need to be interpreted to particular circumstances. This is not the relativity of situationism which says there are no rules and every situation must be judged by its own merit. It is the wise application of a general rule to the specific situation. Zealots apply rules rigidly: too rigidly.

The topic of business ethics is sexy. Companies like to portray themselves as squeaky-clean. And senior managers do lots of integrity and ethical talk. But the reality is often different. And it is the gap, often a yawning chasm, between the hype and the reality that really disillusions staff. Paradoxically, it may be those who talk least about integrity who demonstrate it most often.

Intrinsic motivation

Why is a pilot paid more than a professor? Or a newsreader paid more than a nurse?

There are many glib answers to this seemingly simple and obvious question. Market forces of supply and demand; selection and years of training; a history of trade union bargaining; Hay points.

One factor recognised by everybody is that intrinsically motivating jobs require somewhat less compensation and benefit than extrinsically motivating jobs. But what is the difference? It can be illustrated by the following true story.

A writer was scribbling at home; or at any rate tapping the keys. Things were going well. But being a holiday the local park was full of children laughing and playing. Their erratic, loud, uncontrollable noise was deeply disturbing. And there was no easy alternative for the writer. Closing the windows did little to muffle the sound, only making the room stuffy. There was no other room to decamp to. So what to do, other than, as they say, 'move the children on'.

A number of possibilities arise: threaten the children or bribe them to go away. The method is well-known to the mafia. The children might accept the bribe but soon return to this lucrative source of dosh.

The academic, however, knew his motivation theory. He wandered out, wearing demob corduroy, to confront the noisy interference. Mustering all the charm he could, he gathered the children around him and told them that he had observed them from his office and had admired and enjoyed their noisy games, high-spirited yells and laughter – so much so he was prepared to pay them to continue. Each child was given a pound.

Of course they continued. The wise old don did the same the next day and the next. But on the fourth day he sallied forth and the expectant children gathered around. He explained that for various reasons he had no money so he could no longer continue to 'subsidise' the play. Speaking on behalf of the others the oldest child said that if he thought the children were going to carry on playing for nothing he was sadly misinformed and they 'were off never to return'.

What the writer knew was that the essence of play is that it is intrinsically satisfying. It is a preposterous idea to pay people to play because they love and volunteer for the activity. You only have to recompense people for doing things they do not really enjoy: things that are dangerous or mind-numbingly dreary; things that are tiring or stressful.

A few years ago a psychologist, Mihaly Csikszentmihalyi, wrote a book called *Flow* (1990; HarperCollins) which tried to describe and explain that magical state of pleasure that people get doing a favourite activity. This maybe hiking or hang-gliding; singing the *Messiah* in a full choir or carefully tending a loved garden. They are, for enthusiasts, deeply satisfying experiences; engrossing and enriching; beguiling and very personally rewarding.

Hobbies and pastimes are very varied and quite clearly one man's meat is another's poison. A day at an allotment, an evening fishing by the canal, or morning on the virgin piste is for some heaven and others hell. So is flow a deeply individual experience? Partly; but there are jobs which offer many flow opportunities and those practically none at all.

Consider some really rotten jobs. How about a traffic warden. They are deeply loathed, underpaid, frequently assaulted, out in all weathers, doing something no one respects them for. Or a ubiquitous security guard: unbelievably tedious, occasionally dangerous. Or working on a dreary production line in a noisy, dirty factory.

Two indicators of pay level are how long it takes to master the skill and knowledge to do the job and second the responsibility that go with it. So to return to our example. Training as a pilot takes years and their responsibilities are considerable. Every day they are directly responsible for many hundred human lives.

Most professors do not have that sort of responsibility but their training is usually much longer. The qualifications and teaching experience may be 15 to 20 years before reaching the status.

But how intrinsically motivating is it flying a jumbo jet? The answer is not a great deal. Sophisticated automation has turned pilots into computer monitors. They hardly 'drive the bus' any longer and once the route coordinates have been inputted their job is to watch the dial. Their job is repetitive and the hours long. There might be nice stop-overs but to live with omnipresent jet lag is no fun. Most are not a happy lot as may be observed by their readiness to strike.

Striking professors of course are not unknown, though pretty rare. In Britain, at any rate, they have seen their comparative income decline for most of the century but still there is fierce competition for the job. Why? The answer is intrinsic motivation.

While they have both administration and teaching responsibilities, academics know that it is their research that leads to promotion. And what, where and why they research is left up to them. They may follow their passions and whims, exploit their talents as they feel fit. Labs and libraries are occupied at weekends not out of extrinsic, but intrinsic, motivation. Professors often double their required hours of work, but don't get paid overtime. Indeed the idea is preposterous. It's like paying children to play.

Naturally there comes a point in all deeply intrinsically motivating jobs where people make the choice between lifestyles. People in the City are conspicuously extrinsically motivated. They want high earnings before retirement at 40 (or 50). They are prepared to put up with very long hours of stressful work for lots of money if it allows them to do something intrinsically motivating afterwards.

The really hard question is how to motivate those whose job is not, and probably cannot be, intrinsically motivating. How to motivate a person gutting chickens in a cold factory on a deprived estate?

There are no easy answers but there are things that can be done. These workers often want a sense of belonging and autonomy. So they form self-managed teams. Give them clear goals and guidelines and a lot of help to begin with; but let them decide how they achieve their goals and they do become interested, particularly if there are rewards attached to performance.

You can never make extrinsically motivating jobs as attractive as those with very clear intrinsic features, but something can be done.

Judging intelligence

Job advertisements for a very wide range of jobs at very different levels often specify very similar traits required for the job. These traits or competencies are typically such things as team-player, innovative, customer-focused, honest, hard-working and so on. Surprisingly, intelligence is rarely mentioned, though there may be euphemisms for it.

Of late the academic literature has confirmed what many people knew to be true about the best individual predictors of work success. Using meta-analyses, that is analysis of many other (good) studies, researchers have shown that a limited number of factors at work are highly predictive of work success in general. They are intelligence, stability (that is, non-neuroticism) and conscientiousness.

Most interviewers, be they trained or not, seem pretty happy with the trait/competency approach. The rapid spread of personality tests has meant many managers (not only those of HR) have a considerably enriched vocabulary to describe people. A much smaller number have an idea of the processes and mechanisms by which these personality traits 'work'. There is of course much debate about personality testing with a pendulum showing the popularity of self-report tests swinging back and forth. But intelligence test usage is, and probably always has been, much less popular in business.

This leaves the observer somewhat bemused. Research shows intelligence the best predictor of job success but few selectors measure intelligence. The question is why?

The concept of intelligence, as well as intelligence testing, is a very hot topic within the social sciences as well as in the public in general. Surprisingly, there is considerable agreement among psychologists as to the issue although there are of course mavericks willing to speak out for the opposite side often based more on a need for publicity than science.

The publication of the *Bell Curve* was the latest spur to popular debate. In an attempt to bring some science to the discussion, one of the world's experts on intelligence wrote a piece in the *Wall Street Journal* (15 December 1994). It specified 25 points about what is known about intelligence under five headings: the meaning and measurement of intelligence; group differences; practical importance; source and stability of within-group differences; source and stability of between group differences; and implications for social policy.

Consider five points from that statement:

- 'Intelligence ... can be measured and intelligence tests measure it well. They are among the most accurate (in technical terms, reliable and valid) of all psychological tests and assessments'
- 'While there are different types of tests, they all measure the same intelligence'
- 'IQ is strongly related, probably more than any other single measurable human trait, to many important educational, occupational, economic and social outcomes'
- 'A high IQ is an advantage in life because virtually all activities require some reasoning and decision making ... the odds for success in our society greatly favour individuals with higher IQs'
- 'Intelligence tests are not culturally biased ... rather IQ scores predict equally ... regardless of race and social class'.

But, whatever the experts say, intelligence and intelligence testing is a politically very sensitive issue. Despite having done no reading or research on the topic, let alone do a psychometrically designed test, many lay people feel confident asserting that the concept is meaningless, the tests biased; the whole thing a conspiracy.

The threat of litigation, bad press or alienating applicants is enough to put most companies off using intelligence tests. Added to this far fewer people feel confident about choosing and using intelligence, compared to personality tests. In the jargon of psychometrics, power tests (ability) are used far less frequently than preference tests (personality).

Interestingly, the military are far less coy than businesses particularly in countries where there is conscription. Imagine the problem of being faced with 100,000 new recruits annually. Who should/could become a fighter pilot, a bomb disposal expert, or a cook? The military are well used to using tests and using them wisely. It is of course a life-and-death issue. And they provide most interesting and important data sets for researchers.

This may explain the situation but it still inevitably does not help the selector. It is pretty self-evident that one needs to be *bright enough* for the job. Bright people learn faster and adapt more quickly. You don't have to be as bright if you intend to become an acupuncturist as an actuary; a pharmacist as a physicist ... a director as a supervisor.

So what are the alternatives to the selector who first admits the salience of intelligence but second is hesitant/resistant about using tests?

Some opt for education as a proxy measure. But education is confounded by class. More recently things have got worse through grade inflation and expanding university attendance. Well over 50 per cent of students at British universities got an upper second (2:1) or above. The government wants 50 per cent of the population of young people to go to university. This means in time a quarter of the population will have 2:1 degrees! School grade inflation suffers the same problem.

At least in the past it was easier to differentiate between good, average and bad educational results even if they were only modestly related to intelligence. This now seems much less possible.

What about asking applications to rate their own intelligence? A host of recent studies on self-rated intelligence would caution against this practice. First, there is a robust gender difference showing female humility and male hubris. Females tend to give scores 5–10 points lower than males. Second, when comparing self-estimate to test scores there are very modest correlations around r = .30 even when under 'experimental' rather than applicant conditions. Worse there is evidence of many 'outliers'. These are people who give high estimates with low scores or vice versa. They are in a sense deluded, believing they are much brighter or dimmer than they actually are.

What about using observers as in referees? This may be the best option as long as it is done sensibly. Rather than try and see whether and how referees 'encode' messages about intelligence in their letters it is better to ask them directly. Ideally one would get a rating on a number of scales related to intelligence even if the word itself were not used. Thus they would be asked to say whether x compared to others in the same position was very much less, much less, less, much more, very much more clever, quick on the uptake, bright, sharp and so on. Note that the technique does not have a mid-point scale.

Call it individual difference capacity if you like. But the single best predictor of success at the managerial level remains intelligence. Not emotional intelligence but analytic intelligence. The books that say the opposite have not done their research.

Kickin' arse

Years of research on the personality characteristics of successful chief executives are beginning to yield consistent results and a few surprises. Three findings are neither new nor surprising. CEOs have to be reasonably bright, emotionally stable and hard working. They must be bright enough to understand the business, tumble the numbers, learn new things.

Managers have to be stable. Work can and does lead to stress; amen. It can cause individuals both chronic and acute stress, which in turn can lead to absenteeism, bad decision making and poor interpersonal relations. Managers need to be hardy and stress-resistant. It is all about coping skills and the way people perceive threats.

Call it conscientiousness, dutifulness, diligence, the work ethic or whatever. Managers have to be hard working, stop. Things can't be shirked or delayed. They may on occasions do serious amounts of unpaid overtime. Indeed overtime isn't a managerial concept. Good managers work smart and hard. They have to learn to be efficient and effective and, when the time calls, put the time in.

But there is another personality variable which perhaps is counter-intuitively related to management success. It's called agreeableness, and really successful managers have *low* scores. Agreeable people are appreciative, forgiving, generous, kind, sympathetic and trusting. They are known for their altruism, compliance and modesty. They are tender-minded and straightforward.

Agreeableness is primarily a personality trait of interpersonal tendencies. The agreeable person is fundamentally altruistic. He or she is sympathetic to others and eager to help them, and believes that others will be equally helpful in return. By contrast, the disagreeable or antagonistic person is egocentric, sceptical of others' intentions, and competitive rather than cooperative.

Agreeable people seem socially preferable and psychologically healthier, and it is certainly the case that agreeable people are more popular than antagonistic individuals. However, the readiness to fight for one's own interests is often advantageous, and agreeableness is not a virtue on the battlefield, boardroom or in the courtroom. Sceptical and critical thinking also contributes to accurate analysis in the sciences.

Most CEOs like to portray themselves as highly agreeable, generous benefactors of the arts, caring contributors to charities, concerned motivational leaders, open and trustworthy and modest about their achievements. That takes a lot of spin – and a poor memory. Look at the history of many a famous CEO and you see narcissism and ruthlessness, politicising and a lot of weaving and ducking. To climb the greasy pole in most organisations takes selfishness and guile. And to stay on top requires a lot of what Americans call 'kickin' arse'. Successful leaders need to be firm but fair. They need to 'let go' the inefficient, the lazy, the uncooperative and the change resistant. Organisations staffed with agreeable people tend to be non-profit organisations: too keen on caring and sharing and rather forgetful about getting the job done, or aggressively targeting competitors.

Giving honest, accurate and negative feedback is very hard for most managers. And the more agreeableness you possess the harder this may be. It is one of the reasons why performance management and appraisal systems have a bad name. Agreeable managers are 'softies': they tend to be generous to poor, weak and lazy employees, consequently angering and demotivating the really hard working and sending a message to the least effective that they are OK.

Most managers know what to do when they notice poor performance: confront it immediately; focus on what needs to be done differently rather than what went wrong in the past; give the person the informational, emotional and technical support they need to do the job – and give them a chance. But if all this fails, 'kick arse'.

Managers who are liked and respected are known for their fairness not forgiveness; for their sound judgement more than their sympathy. True, the characteristics people most want in their bosses are honesty and integrity. The trouble with agreeable managers is that they won't bite the bullet when it comes to taking tough action. In bad times people have to be laid off; incompetent people have to be fired; unreliable suppliers have to be replaced. Agreeable managers find excuses and procrastinate. It seems to hurt them more than it hurts their staff to tell them their time is up. And so they lead the business to disaster.

Successful managers are hard-headed, proud, sceptical, competitive. They can and do express their (negative) feelings without guilt or discomfort. Too disagreeable and they are seen as nasty, selfish, b**tards. But too agreeable and they are simply 'too soft' to do what has to be done.

Shrewd CEOs knows that people like their business heroes to be 'good guys' with all those Disney traits of agreeableness. So they set the spin-doctors to work. But don't believe what you read in the papers. Agreeableness neither gets you to, nor keeps you at, the top of the tree. You need to have ability, skill and timing when it comes to 'kickin' arse'.

Knowledge college management

Taxi drivers 'do the Knowledge'. They have knowledge colleges that help them effectively remember the entire London A to Z. This prodigious feat takes two to three years and actually results, so cognitive neuroscience brain imaging has shown, in parts of the brain growing and being more active.

You can spot students of 'the Knowledge' on Sunday mornings on mopeds with clipboards. It is a form of rote learning. They have to remember, names, places and routes. Dozens of roads have the same name in London differing only by postcode. And routes on the map give no indication about one-way streets, long-term diversions, traffic calming devices (designed mainly to infuriate). So it becomes experimental as well as applied learning.

Very little in business involves rote learning. Even in the most technical of jobs rote learning is unusual. And the higher one goes in organisations the more strategic and less technical one gets. So now we are told not that people are our greatest asset but that knowledge is our greatest asset. And that may be in many heads even if they do not know it. So now we have knowledge managers. So what is KM? It has been defined in many ways but the following is a pretty reasonable and sufficient definition:

> The systematic process of finding, selecting, organising, distilling and presenting information in a way that improves an employee's comprehension in a specific area of interest. Knowledge management helps an organisation to gain insight and understanding from its own experience. Specific knowledge management activities help focus the organisation on acquiring, storing and utilising knowledge for such things as problem solving, dynamic learning, strategic planning and decision making. It also protects intellectual assets from decay, adds to firm intelligence and provides increased flexibility. (T. Davenport, *Some Principles of Knowledge Management*, www.bus.utexas. edu/kman/kmprin.htm)

But the actual, crypto, quasi and even real intellectuals have been wading around in this murky pool. The first thing they do is make distinctions. So the first is between data information and knowledge which is pretty self-evident. But as sceptics have wisely noted:

- A collection of data is not information
- A collection of information is not knowledge
- A collection of knowledge is not wisdom
- A collection of wisdom is not truth.

Then there is the difference between different types of knowledge. Consider the following:

1. *Tacit knowledge:* represented by individual or group experience and expertise, is implicit; used for sense making, problem solving and gaining of perspective, and is personal; held within us and rarely documented.
2. *Explicit knowledge:* based on policies, procedures, instructions, standards and results, is readily communicated, often through written documentation, and provides a record of 'organisational or institutional memory'.
3. *Cultural knowledge:* the basis for what we deem to be fair and trustworthy; an underlying comprehension of how we treat new truths and situations, and is often tied to an organisation's vision, mission and overall philosophy.

In a well-known and early book in the area, *Some Principles of Knowledge Management*, Thomas Davenport set out the 10 principles of KM:

1. Knowledge management is expensive (but so is stupidity!).
2. Effective management of knowledge requires hybrid solutions of people and technology.
3. Knowledge management is highly political.
4. Knowledge management requires knowledge managers.
5. Knowledge management benefits more from maps than models, more from markets than from hierarchies.
6. Sharing and using knowledge are often unnatural acts.
7. Knowledge management means improving knowledge work processes.
8. Knowledge access is only the beginning.
9. Knowledge management never ends.
10. Knowledge management requires a knowledge contract.

But does that help at all? Perhaps the first and most fundamental question to ask is this: 'Why don't people (in the same organisation) share information?' There are of course many answers. But perhaps the most common reasons are:

- *Power:* Knowledge is power, expensively obtained, destabilising if simply 'given away'. The keeper of the files is the great controller. Professionalism is about acquiring specialist knowledge – and with it money, power and influence. Hence the powerful resistance not to give it away.
- *Salience:* Even if prepared to share, do people know what knowledge to share, when, where, why and with whom? What is useful? Will they understand it? Will it go out of date?
- *Culture/climate:* The corporate culture (or immediate climate) does not support/facilitate many forms of participation, or sharing. Despite their vision/mission/values statements many organisations are deeply protective of their secrets. We know the story of the people who know the Coca-Cola recipe. They are probably more likely to be the norm than the exception.
- *Time:* Busy people simply don't have the time to do this, particularly in areas where knowledge is changing fast.
- *Language:* Specialist knowledge is associated with complex jargon that even 'native speakers' (that is, specialists) don't know that they are speaking it and becoming impenetrably incomprehensible. Obfuscation through acronym is the end to KM's discussion.
- *Benefits:* There appear only to be costs but no benefits of the sharing process. It appears entirely to be a one-way street benefiting the organisation. In this world of portfolio management and short-term contracts it may be that holding onto one's specialist knowledge is the only way to ensure re-employment.

So what are problems and issues for KM?

1. *Knowledge acquisition*
Where and how to acquire the knowledge most efficiently. This applies to both the individual and the organisation.

2. *Knowledge prioritisation*
How to decide which is the most important knowledge and which is relatively trivial. This may change dramatically over time.

3. *Knowledge categorisation*

How best to group and sort this knowledge into meaningful categories. This presents an enormous problem with retrieval as all personal computer owners know.

4. *Knowledge storage*

Where and how to store knowledge cheaply, efficiently and reliably so that it is easily and efficiently retrievable.

5. *Knowledge creation*

How to use principles of synergy to create 'new' knowledge. This is like getting the knowledge to work for you and far from straightforward.

6. *Knowledge exploitation*

How best to utilise the knowledge that we have so extensively and expensively collected. In many ways this is the hardest bit. It's most fundamental to the whole KM exercise but far from clear. The web means more and more people can easily access all sorts of facts – some of them even true. A more mobile, better educated workforce is less loyal and in small groups more flexible.

Getting to exploit the knowledge of their staff is nothing new. We may have knowledge managers whose task it supposedly is to do this, but what evidence is there that they succeed? Paradoxically, it's the one area in which practical knowledge and know-how are pretty sparse in knowledge management.

Larks and owls

Nearly one hundred years ago educationalists had to make some pretty important decisions about school timetables. When should one schedule Maths and when PE? When are students most attentive and most receptive? Does rote or new learning take place best in the morning or the afternoon?

Conference speakers prefer the post morning-coffee slot: that is the 11.15–12.15 talk. All eschew the post luncheon talk believing people have a 'dip' in their energy, attention at this period, irrespective of the quality and quantity of luncheon.

Some speakers like the first slot, believing in the primacy effect – those who go first are best attended to and received. Others want to be the last, believing in the recency effect – the last person heard receives the best rating (just before the happy sheets).

People also talk about their time-of-day preferences. They talk about being a lark or a night owl. Larks like to get up early – often very early (4–5.30 am) – because they feel best in the morning. Owls feel they wake up at night – the later the better. If an extreme lark married an extreme owl they may almost never meet. Some larks are 'burnt-out' by the time extreme owls get up. And just when owls are feeling their best the larks have been asleep for a number of hours.

One way of understanding time-of-day effects is to look both at flexi-time behaviours and weekend preferences.

Flexitime is a misnomer because people are often totally inflexible about their choice. Early larks come in and leave early – all the time. Late owls prefer to start and stay late. Some people are flexitime larks because of choice, but for others it is a necessity. Choosing to work at night or on shifts may be a function of lifestyle or necessity. Having young children can dictate.

Dutch researchers have discovered the biological reason for the difference between morning types (larks) and evening types (owls), by observing a time difference in their bodies' daily temperature curve. The biological clock, which regulates our body's circadian (that is, daily) rhythms, is located in two small cerebral groups of cells, the suprachiasmatic nuclei. These cells emit chronometric signals to the body so that it synchronises to the time of day. Heart rate, hormone secretion and body temperature, for instance, are adjusted accordingly. The rhythm of the biological clock cannot easily be changed. Evening types who have to work early in the day can get used to this, but during holidays they revert to their evening type behaviour. The biological clock runs two hours earlier in morning types than in evening types. Up to now, it was assumed that personality differences were involved, such as laziness, extraversion or personal lifestyle.

Regular measurements of the daily temperature curve in both types of people under laboratory conditions show that some people always physiologically wake up earlier than others. In a 24-hour economy, it would be possible for these morning and evening types to work at times which suit them best.

Chronobiology can also be assessed by questionnaires. Here are three fairly typical questions:

1. You want to be at your peak performance for a two-hour test which you know is going to be mentally exhausting. You are entirely free to plan your day and, considering only your own 'feeling best' rhythm, which one of the four testing times would you choose?

   8–10 am ☐   11 am–1 pm ☐
   3–5 pm ☐   7–9 pm ☐

2. You have decided to engage in some physical exercise. A friend suggests that you work out twice a week for an hour and the best time for him is 7 am–8 am Bearing in mind nothing else but your own 'feeling best' rhythm, how do you think you would feel?

   In good form   ☐
   In reasonable form   ☐
   Find it difficult   ☐
   Find it very difficult   ☐

3. How long does it usually take before you 'recover your senses' in the morning?

   Less than 10 minutes ☐   11–20 minutes ☐
   21–40 minutes ☐   More than 40 minutes ☐

'Early to bed, early to rise, mucks a man up and he ruddy soon dies ...'

or is it, 'makes a man healthy, wealthy and wise'? An intriguing paper in the 1998 *British Medical Journal* (C. Gale and C. Martyn, December, **317**: 1675–7), partly answered the question. In Britain, 1229 men and women were studied with regard to sleep patterns, income, health, and cognitive function. Those who go to bed before 11 pm and get up before 8 am are defined as larks, while those who go to bed after 11 pm and get up after 8 am are owls. It was found that owls have a higher mean income, that larks were not superior to owls in cognitive performance and health. An interesting finding that came out of this study was that people who spend 12 or more hours in bed have a much higher risk of death than the average person. The lowest death rate was in those who spent 8 hours in bed.

Larks won't be surprised by the finding that owls are richer. Try to get people to come to a serious breakfast meeting as opposed to one that begins at 17.00 and ends at 21.00. Somehow our culture rewards owls more than larks. They start later, eat at a fashionable time and do business when larks are, quite frankly, too pooped. Larks appear too eager, too keen, too junior – just too insane to those wise old owls who know the world is run by those who prefer darkness to light.

Lumpers and splitters; halos and horns

There is a fundamental difference at the heart of the debate among intelligence researchers between what have been called *lumpers* and *splitters*. Lumpers argue for what the experts call *general intelligence*. Arguments are based on the fact, long established, that if you give people a wide range of ability tests people tend to score about the same on each. That is, bright people tend to do well on all the tests and vice versa. Really good intelligence tests, however, still have as many as 16 subtests measuring vocabulary, verbal reasoning, ability to do calculations, spatial ability and so on to improve both reliability and validity.

Splitters on the other hand argue that intelligence is made up of quite distinct abilities that are not necessarily related to each other. Despite weak evidence for their position, the splitters find popular acclamation. Hence 'emotional' intelligence, 'spiritual' and 'successful' intelligence. Popularist educators argue there are as many as eight unique and distinguishable intelligences, such as verbal, mathematical, spatial, body-kinesthetic, musical, intra-personal, inter-personal and naturalistic.

People, particularly the less gifted, love to believe they have untapped intelligence (they are just using a third of their brain) or that while they might be academically short-changed they can easily compensate by their brilliance at another, equally valuable, skill. It is almost as if they want to be labelled idiot savants: less talented people who show exceptional skills or brilliance in some limited field. Idiot savants are, however, very rare indeed.

Educationalists jump on 'new intelligences' as they get discovered irrespective of the fact most are not abilities but learned skills. Thus, despite the fact that the concept of emotional intelligence has been around for over 50 years it has only been recently 'discovered'. Our grandparents talked of charm, our parents of insightfulness, we of social skills, our children of emotional intelligence.

But the point remains academically true and the lumpers have won at least on the data. Careful and exhaustive empirical research supports the point: whilst we can delineate very specific abilities, the evidence suggests 'they go together' in the sense that people who are good at music tend to be good at maths.

However, there are two other distinctions concerning the academic world of intelligence that are perhaps more interesting and important. The first is the distinction between fluid and crystallised intelligence. The distinction is essentially between problem solving ability and knowledge.

Fluid intelligence is that ability to solve new problems such as programming a new video recorder. It takes a bright imaginative person to see connections, think of alternatives and do a strictly logical analysis quickly. Alas, our fluid intelligence peaks young – in adolescence.

Mathematicians, physicists and engineers need a lot of fluid intelligence to do well. It is no surprise that all those child prodigies who get to Oxbridge at 13 and start their degree do maths. They never do history or languages (which require crystallised intelligence) or literature which requires a maturity of understanding of the human condition.

Our fluid intelligence, like our sexual prowess, may peak at about 18 but fortunately our crystallised intelligence keeps going up. This is mainly because of accumulated knowledge and vocabulary. We might consult 16 year olds for help with the computer but they come to us for help with crosswords.

This split between crystallised and fluid intelligence has important business applications specifically in who one works for as well as how to test people. Because crystallised knowledge is a function of education it means that poorly educated people are seriously disadvantaged by certain tests. When testing people from other cultures and poor backgrounds it's always advisable to use tests of fluid intelligence.

On the other hand, long-serving middle managers have hopefully built up a wide knowledge-base that helps them deal with everyday problems. We hear now of knowledge management which became important after the reengineering debacle when hundreds of wise, middle-aged, middle-brow managers were sacked to improve bottom-line business figures. They took with them a valuable but intangible commodity: knowledge. And knowledge that was not easily available on a CD. Knowledge of suppliers' quirks, of customer peculiarities, of the history of systems, of doing things by hand. So they had to be hired back!

A third issue of importance is the distinction between actual (test measured) and estimated intelligence. Most of us know how bright we are. Formal as well as informal education has given us plenty of feedback. We know the difference between ability and effort, between fast and slow learners. Newspapers and magazines are full of quizzes and tests that (fairly accurately) measure intelligence. So we have enough opportunities to know how we 'stack up' against our peers on the bell curve.

There is therefore a significant positive correlation between self-estimated and test-derived intelligence scores. But there are also curious 'outliers': seriously bright people who don't believe they are; and, well, 'less talented' individuals who believe they are somewhat smarter than they actually are. The former are sad; the latter annoying. Research suggests it is more likely for underestimators to be female; and overestimators, male. The sadness of the underestimators is that their lack of self-confidence in their real abilities means that they rarely really exploit their talents. They are often underemployed. They are the victims of the well-known self-fulfilling prophesy – believe you are average or below-average and behave accordingly.

On the other hand, there are the simply deluded: despite evidence to the contrary they believe they are considerably more intelligent than they are. Curiously, the strategy may work and they may never be 'found out' though it is likely their close working companions and support staff (often much brighter than them) do suspect. By careful selection, teamwork and delegation the bluff of the overestimators may work well for them. Some fall foul of the impostors' syndrome, later on actually bringing about their downfall; the majority blunder on.

Certainly underestimators may require more help than overestimators for all our sakes.

Most people in business are rather embarrassed in talking about intelligence. They prefer euphemisms: capacity, skills, abilities. We like to believe, despite the evidence, both that intelligence is not really that important in business and/or that it can be trained. Alas, both are untrue.

Intelligence is the single best predictor of success at work. That's why it's important and deserves serious attention from the business community.

Lying in interviews

Most interviews, particularly those involving selection, witness three interesting psychological and moral phenomena. Self-deception, impression management, and downright porkies. And who tells them? Both inquisitor and applicant: job seller and job buyer. Telling lies at interview is not only an issue for interviewers.

A selection interview is somewhere between a charade, hall of mirrors and theatrical farce. Usually the cast is well rehearsed and the lines delivered faultlessly or melodramatically. In fact both sides may be so involved in being word-perfect they have little left to detect the probity of the other.

Problem number one is *self-deception*. Technically these are untruths told by people who do not know them as such. Most of us know others who genuinely *think* they have a sense of humour. We know, as do practically all their colleagues and family that they are mistaken. But this does not shatter their belief. They behave as if they had, tell others about it, even boast of it. Alas, they deceive not only themselves.

To be deluded about a sense of humour may have relatively few consequences, unless of course, one is applying for job of comedy scriptwriter. But (really) to believe one is bright when average (or worse, dim) or insightful and perspicacious when lacking in that arena is more serious. There may be a number of abilities and traits where people are particularly prone to self-deception. They include courage, creativity, emotional intelligence, flexibility and intuition.

Yet positive self-deception may be less problematic than negative self-deception for the interviewee. Many people know the physically attractive person who appears genuinely to believe they are plain, even ugly. Those unconvinced by their talents, however, are much less a problem at interview as their undeserved, low self-esteem often means they don't even reach the interview in the first place. But beware that charming, donnish, self-deprecating façade that is a clever way of turning humility into hubris. Real self-deceivers don't do that. For all sorts of reasons they have a seriously biased view of themselves.

Self-deception may be an index of something more serious such as narcissistic personality disorder. The fact is that it may serve a person well in business life up to a point and then very suddenly lead to disaster. Those who derail as senior managers are often chronic self-deceivers.

But it is a mistake to believe that self-deception is exclusively the issue for the interviewee. Try being on a selection panel at work to see how your colleagues portray themselves, their department or the organisation as a whole to potential new recruits. For some, it confirms their worst nightmares that marketing believe their own propaganda or that HR *really* did not understand the business.

It maybe unwise to present the organisation, its product and personnel in too positive a light, but it is perhaps more problematic to be self-deceived over its merits. Being too long or too senior in any organisation may not help the self-deception problems of selectors – nor being too narrow in one's speciality and understanding.

Self-deception takes some time to detect. We all expect impression management at interviews. Make-up, the smart suit, the carefully tooled CV, are all part of the impression management process. It really is 'spin for the individual'.

Impression management is about a selective, carefully presented version of the truth. It is about advertising. And as such, the presumption is that the advertiser knows the facts but chooses to present them in a particular way. After a while most people can decode the script. We all know what estate agents mean by 'deceptively spacious', 'designer kitchen' or 'charmingly original'. We also know about the lush vocabulary used by the menu writers. Such as 'pan-fried sea bass chaperoned by market vegetables'.

Impression management is more about sins of omission than commission. It can be about selective amnesia. Candidates know about packaging and presentation. Many prepare as thoroughly as they can. They hire CV designers and professional photographers. They read up about the company. They buy books entitled *Great Answers to Tough Interview Questions*.

But of course it is the company interviewers who buy those tomes called *Killer Questions at Interviews* or *Read People Like a Book*. Organisations eager to attract the bright young things from the best universities indulge themselves in serious impression management. Try observing the milk-round or careers fair.

Individual interviewers are deeply committed to impression management. With panel interviewing they are as eager to show off to colleagues as the candidate. They too dress the part; interview in the newly decorated office; hand out glossy brochures making the organisation look good.

The third problem is as much about *morality* as psychology; lies, damn lies, and interview answers. The golden trio for selection assessments in the application form (CV), the interview and references. Here the applicant and his/her referees are asked direct specific questions about education, job experience and the like.

And it is here that the line between impression management and down-right lies remains blurred. Thus '1994–1996: senior manager sales with £500,000 budget' can mean many things. Under 'Education', people forget to put down things because it does not say all educational qualifications, or put down incomplete degrees because, they argue, it was not specified.

Referees can lie for lots of reasons: they are asked questions when they simply have no data and are too embarrassed to admit it; they are desperate to get rid of the person; or they simply don't care.

Do interviewers lie on behalf of themselves, their section or company as a whole? Really lie: tell untruths, not just 'little white lies'? Probably, but mercifully not that often.

Psychologists are rather good at catching liars in questionnaires. They are not too bad at noticing non-verbal behaviours associated with lying at interview. But self-deception and impression management may take a little longer than an interview to detect. Who needs their advice? Interviewers and interviewees, for they both need the skills. But it is companies, not individuals, that have the money to spend trying to get an accurate assessment of the other in the selection interview. So courses, books and seminars are dedicated to the needs of interviewers. And it becomes mythology that it is only interviewees, not interviewers, who won't or can't tell the truth.

Management apologetics

There is a branch of theology called 'Apologetics': It is not about being contrite, guilty and chanting eternal 'mea culpa'. It is about providing a systematically reasoned argument in defence, and vindication of, (Christian) beliefs. An apologist is therefore one who speaks and writes in defence of a belief system, specific cause, or institution.

For some time, it has been fashionable to be anti-management. The conventional argument is that most organisations would be a lot better off with fewer managers. After all, most simply inhibit and frustrate those doing real work in production and sales. Further, management is not a profession, just commonsensical following intuition and, where that fails, calling in consultants. Disillusion with managers results when they are seen as a lethal mixture of corrupt and incompetent. One response is either to impose more legislation to try to ensure standards are maintained or else use the executive as watchdog. Worse: ask shareholders to reform the job of management through various voting systems. These solutions end in tears.

Managers, the critics say, are (thank goodness) a dying breed on the edge of extinction. This is because they are slow, bureaucratic, hierarchical, inflexible and inadaptable. The big, ponderous, manager-infested conglomeration of old has been replaced by the small, adaptable, mean and lean organisation of today. These new firms operate with only an informal structure, and win by quick, action-orientated and intuitive methods. Less is more managerially.

Elephantine megaliths, the natural home of the middle managers, are as doomed as a Dilbert Dodo. The fleet-footed, high-tech, high-touch, highly adaptable firms are the world of tomorrow. The new employee is a self-managing, portfolio-orientated, multi-talented person in no need of a middle-brow, controlling middle manager.

But what would the apologist say? Paradoxically, it is the gurus teaching in business schools for very expensive MBAs who are the greatest enemies of administrators. So how to defend the indefensible? What arguments can be mounted in defence of management?

- *Defence 1:* Large companies not only persist but increase. Car, insurance, publishing and pharmaceutical companies are growing larger not smaller. Governments start quangos to try to prevent megalithic monopolies.

Companies grow because of the advantage of economies of scale. When companies have tens of thousands of employees someone has to define, direct and coordinate, particularly where standardisation is thought to be important. In fact, the increase in managers is usually modest relative to the increase in the number of employees. And as all armies from all nations for all time have discovered, things such as a *clear chain of command* with a realistic *span of control* and *logical procedures* is simply the best way to get things done.

■ *Defence 2:* Small companies need managers. While entrepreneurial owners are seeking out opportunities, sourcing finance or negotiating contracts, someone has to keep the show on the road. Those who let go the 'hands-on' bit often see the company stall: but to grow means letting go – to the appropriate middle manager. In fact we have known for 50 years that small companies tend to have proportionately more managers than bigger ones. It's the economy of scale argument again.

■ *Defence 3:* As the business world becomes more complex and therefore difficult to administer there are more rather than fewer needs for managerial expertise. Increases in regulation, consumer pressure groups and economic instability require more managerial expertise. A good manager is a tactician, a stabiliser, a morale booster, and so on. We need less regulation and better managers.

■ *Defence 4:* Managers are better educated today than they ever were. Sure, some revel in jargon, others follow fads, some are dogmatic, but they are for the most part better trained. Management might not be a profession in the established sense of the word but there is evidence that general managers are more able, stable and skilled than they have ever been. The body of (real, objective, useful) knowledge about management science is increasing. It is based on core disciplines that include accounting, economics, finance, psychology and law but is changing fast. Sound, reassuringly clear thinking, jargon-free communication and an ethical position are now far more commonplace. We have evidence-based management from bright go-ahead people who want to be, and are proud to be called, managers.

There is nothing wrong with structure: structures imply a set of organising principles, means of communication, lines of report. They need to fit the product, the culture of the times. They can be changed. But only the fool (or management guru) wants an organisation to be structureless. That is clearly the route to anarchy. Good managers are also analytical and thoughtful before becoming action orientated. They need to understand the problem sufficiently before acting on it. They need to master a range of techniques and skills to do the job well. These are acquired through formal and informal learning.

Perhaps the greatest culprit in the demise of the status of the manager is the blockbuster business book written by the academic guru. Management is portrayed as simple: follow a few simple points and you become a great manager. Walk about; throw a few fish about; move your cheese and so on.

Managers, even CEOs, are not very good advocates of their cause when confronted by experienced journalists. Various national management associations do not put in much effective effort, it seems, in improving the image of the much maligned manager.

The public often sees managers as corrupt, obsessed, naive or plain lazy. They are less often portrayed as people wrestling with complex problems in a volatile environment. A generation of middle managers was culled during the downsizing fad or reengineering. It led to tears and capsising.

No amount of spin or PR can save managers their respect or reputation. They have to make serious decisions in the face of uncertainty; they have to separate signal from noise in the data; they have to boost and sustain morale; they have to create a culture of success.

Managers need to be taught in a non-defensive way to articulate their role and contribution. They need to look, and be, up-to-speed, thoughtful and be able to communicate in jargon-free language. In short they need to act like any other professional.

The processes of classical management are not out of date anymore than those of parenting. Managers need their apologists in times of unprecedented criticism. Perhaps management apologetics should be top of the curriculum at all good business schools.

Management literacy

The word literacy has clearly been hijacked. It used to have a simple and clear meaning which referred to the ability to read. Countries have literacy statistics which are proud boasts of their economic and democratic development.

But now we have *computer literacy* and *media literacy*. Governments want people to be *economically literate* so that they can make wise decisions about their futures and take responsibility for their own lives.

Social psychiatrists now talk about *psychiatric literacy*. What they mean is the ability of the general public to recognize mental illness in general. Can people spot a panic attack of a phobic or a delusional state of a schizophrenic? Do they see the manic phase of a bipolar sufferer as 'normal' or not? Can they differentiate a narcissistic personality disorder and paranoid psychosis?

Various mental health charities and support groups are particularly interested in educating the general public about specific disorders. They hope to demystify, de-demonise and educate at the same time. They want people to be compassionate rather than fearful. They want lay people to favour therapy and integration rather than punishment and isolation.

The lay public remain stubbornly uninformed about mental health issues. The information is more likely to come from sensational soaps and Hitchcock horrors than research.

Despite their impressive understanding and use of the communication media, it is possible that young people are no better informed than their parents about the causes of alcoholism, the incidence of autism, or the (lack of) cure for Alzheimer's.

Some organisations appear to have increased awareness for particular syndromes and disorders even if this has led middle-class parents to become a little overenthusiastic about seeing ADHD, dyslexia and so on in their offspring.

But what about *management literacy*? Most managers need to be literate in four areas. First they need sufficient *knowledge of their specialty*. Lawyers need to know about the law, engineers about engineering, marketers about marketing and HR managers about, well, human behaviours.

Next they all need basic *financial competence*. Hence the popularity of courses called 'Finance for non-financial managers'. Financial literacy is necessary in all jobs, the more so the higher one flies. Understanding cash flow, balance sheets, pricing and labour costs becomes significant.

Third, managers need to understand their *business* – that is, the peculiarities of their sector, product and clients. Though there may be some important similarity across sectors, such that managing an airline may be little different from managing a shipping company, and managing a clothing retailer not that different from managing a food retailer, there are numerous business peculiarities one needs to fully understand: the supply chain, the demography of clients, market share, and so on.

But there is a fourth and often overlooked literacy. It may be called *people literacy* or *psychological literacy*. It is about understanding oneself and others. The popularity of the rather muddled concept of emotional intelligence attests to the importance of the idea.

Ask 100 people if they had to choose a boss with high IQ and low EQ, or the other way around. A surprisingly large majority choose EQ. We have all come across the gauche, boorish, nerd-like boss, completely insensitive to the needs of those around him (and it's nearly always a 'him' not a 'her'). They forsake people for policy, morale for machines, emotions for engineering, because they find the latter easier.

Psychological literacy used to be called social skills. There used to be courses that dealt with non-verbal communications, assertiveness, motivation and counselling. They taught useful but transferable skills and helped a lot of managers.

The good news is that psychological literacy can be taught. Like all the other literacies, people can learn to be more perceptive, emphatic and inspiring. Not everybody learns at the same pace but, more importantly perhaps, not everybody believes he/she needs to learn, practise or use the skills. Remember it only takes one psychologist to change a light bulb but it needs to want to be changed.

The problem with general management is that those who seem good at financial literacy are weak at, and downplay, psychological literacy, and vice versa. But for true management literacy one needs both.

Management tips

Tipping is not a trivial business. It is estimated that over 90 per cent of restaurant diners tip their waiter/ress around the tune of 10 per cent of the bill. If you include part-timers there may be as many as a million people employed in the serving business. Often a substantial portion of their income is based on tips. So it pays to learn how to maximise the tips.

It may seem petty or pointless or indeed a waste of the tax payers' money, but social scientists have indeed researched the tipping process. The results of their studies can be found in such august and widely read journals as the *Cornell Hotel and Restaurant Administration Quarterly*!

The researchers have concentrated on those behaviours that maximise customer tips. The research is rigorous enough and potentially important in understanding customer service in general. For once it is easy to measure satisfaction: hard currency/cash. Further, one can systematically vary particular behaviours to try to ensure that each specifically relevant behaviour, and its outcome, is examined.

What the research has shown is that some things systematically work and others do not. These results have implications for all service business. Why we tip waiters, hairdressers and taxi drivers but not nurses, shop assistants and tradespeople is unclear and much debated. Nevertheless, the findings are equally applicable to them, and all service businesses.

Three classes of variable seem to predict tipping. There is a class of *interactional behaviours* that do impact on tipping though some of these American studies might not replicate exactly among the stuffier, more introverted and sceptical British. A whole range of waiter/ress behaviours have been demonstrated to have a modest but noticeable effect on tips because of the personalising of the service. These behaviours include:

- *Touching* the customer discreetly, lightly and in a neutral part (forearm while laying the napkin)
- *Squatting* during initial contact at the table to ensure eye contact is at the same level, or preferably where the (all) powerful customer is higher than the lowly server waiter/ress
- Making additional *'non-task' visits*, but discreetly and in moderation, just to check that all is well and nothing extra is required
- *Smiling* warmly and genuinely when greeting the customer and being pleasant, optimistic

- Introducing themselves *by name* also helps to personalise the service. It works much better than having a name badge
- Even implicit factors like *writing thank you* or *drawing a cartoon* on the bill works – well, at least in America.

The mechanism is that appearing helpful, positive, warm and friendly makes a big difference. We know that: sure, so why are so many waiting staff surly, eye-contact avoidant and miserable when they can control these factors? Have they not read the literature? Have they never been a restaurant customer themselves? Is the game not worth the candle? Perhaps not.

A second factor is absolutely crucial, easy to predict but not always within the control of the server – *speed*. A threefold speed of response is important: speed of delivery of drinks, menu and actual food order; speed of delivery of the food; and perhaps most importantly speed of delivery of the bill. The last may be most important as it most closely impacts on the customer's mood as he/she dishes up the dosh.

It's more about optimal speed than maximal speed. Waiters who are too eager to turn you out through lightening quick service and continually filling your glass from your bottle of wine are as unpleasant as those who disappear, dither or delay. The trick is to understand what the customer wants and the clues are not too difficult to read. The business lunch may be quick or slow: get the timing right and the tip increases.

Next is the *free gift approach:* the complementary, mouthfull-size aperitif as one is sipping the drinks; the truffle with the bill. If you believe in the primary effect (first impressions count), you place the gift early on; if you believe in the recency effect (that which came last/most recently has more effect), you place the gift at the end.

The idea is that gifts are reciprocated. Most people feel obliged to reciprocate acts of generosity even if those acts were not requested or anticipated. That is how wine tasting works: get less than 50 pence worth of wine 'free' and people are prepared to pay pounds per bottle over the price they could get elsewhere.

There are service factors beyond the control of the waiting person and restaurant management. Tips have been shown to be in part a function of the *weather:* sunny day → happy mood → more generous. They are some-times a function of whether guests *drink:* more alcohol → less rational judgement → bigger tips. They are always a function of the size of the *party*: more people → proportionately less tips.

Tips are sometimes about chemistry. Customer fancies serving person and tries to impress/bribe them. Occasionally serving people talk about insecure men trying to impress others (often their female guest) by a munificent tip.

Tips are also about fulfilling expectations about the quality and quantity of food, the ambience of the restaurant and the cost that is all beyond the control of serving staff.

Of course excellent food helps. And naturally more expensive restaurants attract more 'high rollers' who have more money to slosh about.

The moral of the story is this: studies on tipping provide useful tips for management on what customers value and want and therefore how to train and reward service staff in all industries.

Marketing hubris and humility

Human resources specialists are used to critical self-examination of their role, function and even existence. Derided as bureaucratic, unresponsive, self-important, 'Human Remains' they are practised at personnel apologetics: a defence of their importance in the organisation.

Accountants, engineers and IT specialists don't bother with all this function justification nonsense. They have confidence that they are central and indispensable to the organisation.

The marketing specialists fall somewhere between the two. To some outsiders, marketing is all about flimflam, expenses and brand-babble. They appear to do little themselves, instead subcontracting creative agencies to undertake all the hard work. And, in that cosy relationship, the marketers like to be lunched and invited to shoots in exotic locations, as brand experts.

Focus groups, mood boards and brainstorming are neither new nor rocket science. Up to half of the money spent is wasted: a fact admitted by all advertising experts. Some products sell themselves. So what's the point of marketing?

Despite their smart suits, smooth talk and irrepressible self-confidence, occasionally the marketing fraternity indulge in a bit of self-critique. But like a summer shower it does not last long. They tend to be natural optimists, not gloomy self-absorbed pessimists.

What do marketers claim as their special area of knowledge and expertise? First and foremost they claim to understand their consumers. They should know about the demographic and psychographic changes in society. Families and households have changed dramatically. Immigration has led to distinct ethnic groups. Children are richer, more demanding and with more savvy.

Consumers are coy, capricious and irascible. They can be fickle and disloyal; no more so than adolescents. What is 'cool' one day, is quite literally 'boring' the next. Hence, there are 'ologists' of one sort or other who 'chase cool' just as Midwestern sensation seekers chase tornados.

Unlike quasi- and crypto-political groups who supposedly speak 'on behalf' of consumers as a whole, marketers know this is quite impossible. Indeed, they spend all their time segmenting markets into groups with funny titles such as 'grey wolves', 'aspirationals', 'macho blokes', 'belongers and emulators'. They argue that these different groups are driven by very different needs and hence need products aimed at them specifically.

Marketers are fascinated by everything to do with branding: names, colours, associations. Many have near mystical beliefs in the powers of branding. The more extreme may hire 'depth psychologists' to tease out curious counter-intuitive associations with brands. They see themselves as guardians of the brand, even masters of corporate social responsibilities.

Second, marketers claim to understand the fuzzy business of communication: namely how to advertise and market the product. Perhaps the media are changing even faster than the consumers themselves. The media are more segmented and buying media is much more complex. Communication is about the medium and the message as well as the audience and placement. Where, when and how to get more bang for your buck is crucial. It may be more art than science, more guesswork than actuarial work, but still very important.

Third, marketers have to be good at interpersonal skills. They have to interact with, persuade and charm people from the City, foreign suppliers, consultants, colleagues; even customers. Financiers, buyers, suppliers, retailers and customers are all part of the fuzzy remit of those in marketing.

Marketing hates to be confused with sales as if they were equal and equivalent. Marketing sees itself as having a much wider remit than mere sales. Nevertheless, marketers have to charm, persuade and encourage the hail-fellow-well-met types in the sales force.

Fourth, marketers have to study, understand and predict the behaviour and fortunes of their competitors. They do this through research, often akin to industrial espionage, which is all part of the great game of marketing. And the skills required may be considerable.

In Britain, most CEOs seem to come from a background in finance. It is accountants who really understand the business, or so they would have us believe. They may be low on emotional intelligence, poor communicators and more instinctively 'costs down' than 'revenue up', but they seem to make it to the top.

In America, on the other hand, many big-time CEOs rise through the marketing route. Perhaps it's understanding communication and 'the vision thing' that appeals to our transatlantic cousins. Marketing people also know the business: they are involved with governments and suppliers, customers and staff, partners and consultancies. They should understand pricing and margins; sales and manufacturing; customers and strategy. Hence, unlike their HR cousins, they often have a good grasp of the whole business. No wonder they are not prone to self-doubt.

Money secrecy

Should people in an organisation know precisely what each other are paid? Should they know roughly, given published wide bands for particular job levels (for example Senior Supervisor £25,000–£29,000)? Or should the amount be a secret known only to a select few, who are themselves sworn to secrecy?

It is not clear if this is a business ethics issue. Certainly it seems that the 'politically correct' option would favour openness and honesty.

But there are good reasons to favour the judged middle option of publishing vague indicators or bands rather than precise amounts. Of the other two options, secrecy is by far the best given that one wants a quiet life.

The problem lies in *perceived equity*. All of us favour the equity principle which suggests that reward (that is, money) should be a function of effort and ability. Your outputs should reflect your inputs. Work harder, have more responsibilities, possess more skills and you get better rewarded.

The equity principle is at the heart of the performance management ideology. Performance-related pay is a way of establishing equity where two people in the same job and with the same experience, through differential effort and dedication, succeed in producing very different outputs. It has been known since the 1920s that the best worker often produces three times as much as the worst.

People at work are very sensitive to social comparisons. Their pay satisfaction is comparative, not absolute. It's not the actual amount of money per se that they earn but the amount compared to those above or below them, and more particularly their peers of similar rank in others parts of the organisation or other sites.

Many a strike occurred in the bad old days because workers on dreary assembly plant A discovered that their co-workers, at even more dreary plant B, were paid a penny an hour more. It was 'the principle of the thing'.

Social comparisons are continuous, subtle and invidious. We do it all the time. We all know those of our peers who are skivers and we also know those who are the embodiment of the work ethic. We know those with raw talent and those of modest abilities. Because of the quality and quantity of contact we know all about them.

As a result, we can become deeply disillusioned if it is apparent that everyone is paid exactly the same: that is, irrespective of their effort and output. The easiest way for the more productive to render the situation equitable is to reduce their efforts and output to that of the least productive worker.

But we also make upward comparisons. We know all about our bosses. We are, after all, victims of their management styles. We know their foibles and quirks, their strengths and 'development opportunities'. We see and experience their personalities at close hand.

Is one's boss's salary commensurate with his/her abilities, responsibilities and output? Certainly, obsessions with 'fat cats' suggests this is not the case. We read manifest stories about characters at the top who receive salaries 10, sometimes 20 times one's own, but it is patently apparent they don't deserve it in the sense that it is inequitable. They are clearly not 20 times cleverer, harder working or more productive.

But do people fully understand their boss's job? Do they see or understand the issues and problems? Do they understand the responsibilities and accountabilities and the stress costs? It is easy to examine outputs and, if they are published, salaries. The inputs are more difficult to see for those above in the hierarchy. But comparatively few people would refuse promotion – almost everyone believes that the extra pay is worth the extra burdens.

Of course, pay is just part of the 'package'. Holidays, privileges, cars and perks are usually commensurate with salary and position. Whatever the money secrecy situation, these added benefits are pretty observable.

The situation is really quite simple. You cannot stop social comparisons, but you can avoid, in part, the problems they cause by not publishing salaries. Publication benefits no one and the costs are too high. Some will argue their beliefs about openness and honesty. All they end up doing is opening a can of worms.

This is not an argument against paying people market rates or against equity theory. People will soon 'vote with their feet' if they undertake social comparisons with others in comparable job and find their own package wanting. But it is an argument in favour of reducing unhealthy, unnecessary and unproductive social comparison processes.

Money is a taboo topic in our society. Keep it that way.

The M-word

Morale is somehow an old-fashioned word. It was the thing senior officers enquired of their subalterns: 'How's morale with the troops, Archie?' The dictionary definition implies three important things about morale. First, it is both a 'mental *and* emotional condition': that is, morale in medieval language is located in both the head and the heart. Second, this condition has various components such as confidence, enthusiasm *and* loyalty. Third, it can be both the property of individuals *and* groups with respect to their job or immediate task.

Morale is one of those old-fashioned words like fortitude, stamina or stoicism that business gurus and writers do not use. The academics have debated a number of things: Is morale an emergent characteristic of the group as a whole? Does morale affect productivity? Morale seems to imply something about energy versus lethargy: is that important? Are some people carriers of good or poor morale, that is, are there healers and poisoners? The academics prefer other labels to morale. They talk, perhaps pretentiously, of organisational commitment, perceived distributive and procedural justice, intrinsic and extrinsic motivation and leadership consideration.

Organisational commitment is the opposite of organisational alienation. It's about feeling loyal to the organisation because it seems loyal to you. They care so you care. Commitment comes from the head and the heart: it is both rational and emotional. The term commitment can have both positive and negative connotations. One is committed to a mental hospital after committing an offence. On the other hand a marriage is a ceremony of 'loving commitment'. Commitment is about binding, through thick and thin. It's about the long haul: not being mercurial or fickle. Morale, like commitment, endures. But it can be broken and, if so, is not easy to repair.

Morale is also linked to the concept of fairness. Nothing lowers morale more than nepotism, favouritism or corruption. People have a strong need to feel equitably dealt with: they need to feel that effort and output will be fairly rewarded. Distributive justice is about how rewards are distributed; pay, promotion and perks are a function primarily of productivity. The able, the motivated and the conscientious do well. It provides a level playing field. Secretive favouritism is the enemy of morale. Few people resent unequal rewards as long as they are equitable.

Procedural justice also affects morale. This is about *how* decisions are made rather than *what* decisions are made. It is the 'trial by jury' ideal; the idea that there are processes and procedures with checks and balances, that ensure good and wise decisions are made. Again, morale is soon destroyed by the kangaroo court; the smoky secretive room where unaccountable and unexplained decisions are made.

Morale in any group has a great deal to do with a person's motivation for staying in the group, and for believing in the purpose of the group. Work groups have a cause, a function, a purpose. The more one is intrinsically motivated by that, the easier it is to maintain morale. Religious and political groups can endure substantial setbacks because of their intrinsic motivation. The volunteer is worth ten conscripts. Believers in the cause certainly have more resilient morale.

Morale is both the property of individuals and groups. Ask people about their personal morale, that of their (smallish) work group, their department and that of the organisation as a whole and you see a clear pattern. Climate surveys invariably show that most people believe they have good morale, as do their personal work friends and colleagues, but they are pretty unsure about the department. And they certainly believe that overall company morale is low and probably steadily declining. In the eyes of workers, morale seems to dissipate across, down and up organisations. One reason for this is that morale is a function of social contact.

Individuals' basic level of optimism (versus pessimism), and their emotional stability are relevant factors. The hardy optimist will have more resilient morale than the neurotic pessimist. Powerful individuals can palpably affect group morale either way. The 'Job's comforter' types can break it; the Churchillian patriotic type can sustain it. No wonder then that groups often have two leaders: the strategic thinker and the socio-emotional manipulator. Groups often develop very effective rituals to cope with the morale problem. But once morale is broken it is difficult to repair.

They used to talk of Moral Rearmament. The CEO of a new M&A or a failing company is, quite wisely, equally interested in morale rearmament. Some discover that it's pretty difficult to turn vicious into virtuous cycles such that a declining morale (and productivity) is reversed.

Is morale a cause or consequence of productivity and success? Probably the causation goes both ways; good morale reflects success and in part sustains it. It's worth monitoring and paying attention to. All good leaders know that. Whatever you might call it, morale is a good dipstick for health of any company.

Nomadic workers

There are many fundamental differences between agrarian and nomadic societies. Nomads are usually forced, through environmental extremes, to be hunter-gatherers or shepherds, moving in search of good pastures and better weather. The Eskimos or Inuit, some sub-Saharan Arabs and the Kalahari Bushmen are constantly on the move. They have a way of life suited to this necessity.

The closest equivalent to this in the West are the gypsies or travellers who restlessly move around. Their long history and culture should not be confused with the new travellers, whose peripatetic wandering seems as much about escaping mundane reality as anything else.

Nomadic societies socialise their children into the values and skills they need to survive. They develop mores and social norms that help their people adapt. They value independence and perseverance and teamwork, which is a life and death issue. They are very hospitable to other nomads. Agrarian societies are geographically stable. They value conformity and tend to be very territorial. In social science this is called ecological determinism. The idea is that the physical environment (climate, terrain, flora, fauna) determines the community maintenance systems (economy, settlement patterns, social structure, division of labour), which determine how children are socialised (caretakers, teachers, tasks) and so how individuals develop their needs, drives, beliefs and values.

So what has this got to do with the world of work? The answer is that work in 'first world' economies is becoming more nomadic. In the past in Western societies, there were nomadic workers: tinkers, seasonal fruit pickers and peripatetic teachers. But they were the exception, not the rule. People went to the office where they had to learn to stay.

Most people at work had no choice but to be agrarian. They were a settled people, with offices or machines that they used to produce their crops of products or services. And, being geographically fixed, they had to learn the ways of the agrarian people, which were about defending their space/property; getting used to hierarchies; obeying the strict conformist rules of the culture. People at work did not have the option of being nomadic: the technology tied them to their desks and machines. But things were going to change. Technology has liberated people from their working environment. People are not tied down to their machines, their desks or their workbenches anymore. They can choose to be nomads.

The fountain pen, well before the ball point, was the first tool to allow movement. Dickensian clerks were tied down by their inkwells. Even if theoretically portable, it was clumsy and inky accidents were common. The boss with the fountain pen could write anywhere. Portability was power. The Mont Blanc confidently showing off its snowy cap in the top inner pocket of the executive still has cachet.

Over time, many of the technologies that tied a worker down became portable. The portable typewriter meant people could work at home, though early models were hardly easily transportable. The field telephones carried by soldiers in the Second World War literally weighed a man down. Early mobile phones, the size of a brick, now seem impossibly ugly and clumsy.

The mobile phone, the car and laptop have untethered people, who now wander about. And the new technologies have exposed the inefficiencies in the old technologies. We know that nearly 75 per cent of phone calls to the fixed phones fail because the person is not there. We know that people may spend around 300 hours a year just listening to their voice-mail.

It is not only portable, wireless (cordless) technology that has unleashed the workforce. Companies have began to realise the costs and cost-savings potential of their large properties and have encouraged their core and contingent workers to 'go home'; leave the nest; become nomads.

The career is dead; the office is dying; headquarters may become virtual. And so an agrarian people have had to become nomadic. There are many who enthuse over the freedom that the peripatetic lifestyle brings. But equally there are others who have serious concerns living in the new electronic life.

Many talk of the stress of being always contactable, never off work. Others note the new health and safety issues concerned with the new technology, such as repetitive strain injury. There are, of course, security issues with hackers. Added to this is the new electro-junk email deluge.

But most difficult of all is adapting to a quite different lifestyle. For the first time, people at work experience the loneliness of the long-distance salesperson, the on-callness of the local doctor and the uncertainty of the fisherman.

The values of nomads are only slowly being introduced to the workplace. Culture change is slow, difficult and painful. It will take a long time for things to stabilise. It certainly brings to life the old idea of 'managing while wandering around'.

Optimism

What leads people to being remorselessly, almost naively, optimistic while others maintain a gloomy pessimistic outlook under the most favourable conditions? Certainly observations confirm that people are fairly consistent over time with respect to their disposition to view the world. In short, optimists nearly always see events (present and future) in a positive light while pessimists see the same events in the opposite way. Optimists see the donut; pessimists the hole.

To the pessimist, an optimist is simply naive: cheerful people blissfully unaware of what is going to happen to them. They lack experience of real life. They enjoy the joke about the first line of Kipling's 'If'. 'If you can keep your head when all about you are losing theirs and blaming you … you clearly have not understood the seriousness of the situation.' It was the famous British sex-researcher Havelock Ellis who noted that the place where optimism most flourishes is in a lunatic asylum. Optimists seize the day; they fill crosswords in with ink.

H.L. Menker said a pessimist was someone who, when smelling flowers, looks round for a coffin. All those in customer-relations, be they doctors or dons, know about the 'heart-sinking' patient/student who is depressed, gloomy and negative. Pessimists suck the energy, the life, the vitality out of one. Pessimists are cautious: they look both ways when crossing a one-way street. And they believe if there is a light at the end of a tunnel it is an oncoming train. They do not inspire others; precisely the opposite.

But to the central question: is one born an optimist/pessimist or is it learnt? The learning option at least offers the possibility of change. Hence the irony that optimists see their disposition as learnt, pessimists as something they are born with. Optimists like to believe things can become better; pessimists know that they can't.

A lot of psychotherapy is about changing patients' views of the world because those views are often seen as self-fulfilling. If you believe nothing can be done; nothing will be done. It goes without saying that pessimists are prone to depression. Inevitably optimism/ pessimism or happiness/unhappiness is a function both of nature and nurture. The nature 'bit' has been known about for well over two millennia when the Greek philosopher Galen identified the four humours: sanguine, phlegmatic, choleric and melancholic.

The *sanguine* type is cheerful and optimistic, pleasant to be with, comfortable with his or her work. The sanguine type has a particularly abundant supply of blood (hence the name sanguine, from sanguis, Latin for blood) and so also is characterised by a healthful look, including rosy cheeks.

The *choleric* type is characterised by a quick, hot temper, often an aggressive nature. The same refers to bile (a chemical that is excreted by the gall bladder in aid to digestion).

The *phlegmatic* person is characterised by their slowness, laziness and dullness. The name obviously comes from the word phlegm, which is the mucus we bring up from our lungs when we have a cold or lung infection.

Finally, there's the *melancholy* temperament. These people tend to be sad, even depressed, and take a pessimistic view of the world. The name has, been adopted as a synonym for sadness, but comes from the Greek words for black bile.

In modern terminology these four types are better understood in terms of two well-known dimensions of personality: extraversion and neuroticism. The sanguine are stable extraverts, the phlegmatic stable introverts. Choleric people are unstable extraverts and melancholic unstable introverts.

There is now considerable, unequivocal evidence from around the world to show personality is strongly related to long- and short-term happiness. And happiness and optimism go hand-in-hand just as much as pessimism and long-term unhappiness.

And there is also equally impressive evidence to suggest that personality is 'hard-wired'. Indeed pundits say personality tests may soon be replaced by mouth-swabs because in the next few years we will have such a good grasp of the neuro-anatomy and pharmacology of personality we shall be able to measure it that way more reliably.

Of course the implications are that to a large degree optimism and pessimism are disposition, stable across time and situations. Inevitably, life events can change optimism and pessimism. Illness, job or relationship problems can certainly dent an optimist's sunny outlook. Less common is to see a pessimist change as a function of positive events. All therapists will attest to the problem of changing the pessimist. It is possible, but only if they want to change.

Groups with opposite experiences, such as quadriplegic patients after injury and lottery winners, return to their initial levels of optimism or pessimism within a couple of years.

So personality, which is closely related to happiness and optimism, is hard-wired and stable. Paradoxically then the pessimists are right; you can't do much about your outlook whatever you are!

Personality testing

Almost no job applicant or training course attendee can escape the ubiquitous psychological test. Such tests are supposed to facilitate the decision making of selectors and the self-insight of trainees. There are psychological test *junkies* who seek out every opportunity to go for yet another test, while there are equally numerous *test-phobes* who would do a great deal to avoid having to be tested. From a tester's viewpoint, there are cynics, sceptics, enthusiasts and addicts whose attitudes to, and use of, tests may be polar opposites.

But what are psychometric tests and how do they work? A few simple clarifications. First, 'psychometric' means 'psychometrised' or 'evaluated' for features such as reliability and validity, which are crucial. However, many tests have not been through such a process. The 'Are you a demon or dodo under the duvet?' tests found in popular magazines have no known psychometric properties. They are devised by journalists, not statisticians. Their aim is to amuse not measure.

Next, tests are crudely divided into tests of power and those of preference. The former are essentially ability tests with right or wrong answers. They may measure general intelligence or specific abilities and are often timed. The score is such that more is good, less is bad.

But preference tests, at least in theory, have no evaluative dimension, for they measure personality or values. In fact we all know that it is better to be stable than neurotic, conscientious rather than indolent. It is debatable whether it is better to be an extravert than an introvert: but most of the literature on happiness and confidence supports that position.

So how are these tests constructed and how do the answers to 20 questions determine if one is an introvert or extravert? It should be noted at this point that most tests give one's score on a single dimension and do not specify types. Hence, most people are neither introverts nor extraverts but ambiverts, because the scores are normally distributed.

Most personality dimensions such as introvert–extravert, or stability–neuroticism have a long lineage. The 'four humours', with all that black and yellow bile, go back to the Greeks. Galen talked about four types: the sanguine (Americans) stable extraverts, the phlegmatic (British) stable introverts, the melancholic (French) unstable introverts and the choleric (Italians) unstable extraverts.

Personality test construction should start with a theory about the origin and structure of personality. Current theories are biologically based: personality is largely inherited and differences are explained by biological processes. Biology is destiny. Personality is 'hard-wired'. The theory should then specify a mechanism or a process which leads people to behave in specific ways.

Thus we have extraversion–introversion linked to cortical arousal. Extraverts are under stimulated and seek out stimulation while the opposite is true of introverts. Thus extraverts choose work and leisure pursuits to achieve excitement, variety, novelty. They like people-orientated activities because people are different, unpredictable, amusing. Their preferences for pharmaceutical stimulants, legal and illegal, reflect their needs for highs, kicks, thrills. The theory says extraverts trade off accuracy for speed; hence they are more error and accident-prone.

Once one has identified the mechanism, it is possible to see distinct but related features of extraversion. Thus we have what are called primary factors under the super-factor of extraversion. These include things such as sociability, impulsivity, assertiveness, positive affect. Once these have been identified and clarified it is time to write individual items. So to measure sociability, the test constructed might aim to identify *five* or so *behaviours* of those high and those low on sociability. These in turn become the individual questions. Note two things: first these questions are usually, but not exclusively about behaviour, though they may test preferences; second, more importantly, some must be reversed (R). So for example:

1. I can really get a party going
2. I enjoy meeting new people
3. I much prefer one-on-one meetings than groups (R)
4. I often crave excitement
5. I sometimes fail to assert myself as much as I should (R)

If there are 5 primary factors associated with extraversion, one needs 5x5 questions to obtain a reliable and robust score. That is why people feel some questions or themes are repetitive. Further, they believe, quite erroneously, that testers try to catch liars by checking inconsistency in answers.

In fact, one catches liars by having a separate lie scale with questions such as 'I always wash my hands before a meal'; 'I have never been late for an appointment'. Tests also catch liars by asking people to choose between alternatives.

Once one has a theory, a draft questionnaire and a scoring system, the difficult bit really begins. This is first demonstrating test reliability, which is usually done by the test retest method. Do a test at time 1 and check scores against a retest at time 2. If you are measuring reliability or validity you should get pretty similar scores.

Next test validity. Do scores predict behaviour logically and significantly? This is the hard bit and the bit which really takes time. There are, in the jargon, many types of validity (called content, construct, concurrent, discriminant, incremental) but the one most test users want is simply predictive validity. This means do test scores predict actual behaviour: does the test actually measure what it says it is measuring? In the business world this means, for instance, does the test score on neuroticism predict absenteeism and does extraversion predict customer ratings of friendliness?

But it is at this point that the long journey to produce a good test stumbles. And it is not because tests don't work. Paradoxically it is usually because organisations do not keep accurate, aggregated, reliable measures of work performance that may be used as the predicted criteria. Do personality tests predict work behaviour? The answer is yes but it depends on which test and which behaviour you are considering. However, if organisations do not actually measure work output well, there is no way tests can be shown to be valid.

Problems of the board

Executive teams frequently have problems. These can be both chronic and acute. And for some the prognosis is poor unless something drastic is done quickly and rationally.

If is often crucially important that the executive team is fit, focused and functional. The dysfunctional team can, in a surprisingly short time, lead an organisation into terminal decline. Shareholders know this to their cost.

What are the typical problems of executive teams and how to deal with them? A number are immediately identifiable. The first is *bloated membership*. Everybody wants to 'sit on the board' and be 'on the top team'. It has been said that the only thing worse than not being on the board is being on the board.

There is an optimal number for an efficient team: somewhere between 7 and 12. Too big and they split; a few become silent and others very vocal. Any CEO needs to be clear about who is on the board *and why* and resist the cancerous growth of those who feel, want or believe they deserve to be at the heart of power. The solution: be clear about membership, limit to an optimal number, and where necessary.

It is, of course, also very important that those on the board bring their expertise and ability but just as much their motivation to succeed through appropriate cooperation. It is all very well having the optimal number but unless they pull together in the process the board will not succeed.

The second is the *naked ambition* of the many team members. Many yearn for the top job; head honcho. They see their career clocks ticking and feel the urge for the money, power and prestige of the top job. There is no easy solution to dealing with the pathologically ambitious. But at least bringing succession planning out into the open helps control some blind ambition. The teams need to specify a timetable, personal criteria for the top job and the process by which the boss is appointed.

It is important the process is open and apparently fair. Nepotism, pusillanimous chair-people, even laziness are reasons for massive board-room squabbling. Having 'nights of the long knives' does no one any good.

The third is *conspiracy of silence*. Surprising perhaps, big boys often cope with issues by never mentioning them. Just as talk about money and death may be taboo in certain circles, teams often deal with emotional issues by ignoring them. As parents attempt to control a five year old's first attempts at shock-swearing by selective deafness so boards often refuse to discuss issues – these may be around success planning, personal pathology, relationships at work or the future of the company.

It is surprising how powerful adults resort to such primitive coping strategies to deal with issues.

The way to stop groups conspiring to be silent is to bite the bullet and, where appropriate, put the issues on the table. There needs to be a rule about what can and cannot be discussed, when and why. It is often the personal pathology of the CEO that dictates what is taboo or not.

Consultants who deal with top-team pathology or boardroom malaise are often astounded by the history 'non-discussables'. Interestingly, it is often tough professional women – so often missing from boards – who deal with the problem best. It is an issue of EQ not IQ … and real balls.

A fourth issue is *resisting centrifugal forces*. Board members can, quite literally, head off in different directions. Their values/priorities can soon lead to the executive team losing its cohesiveness and focus.

This is most frequently the problem where individuals have difficulty delegating. Thus directors manage, managers supervise, supervisors deliver. Delegation should liberate board members to concentrate on what they do: strategy, the vision thing, and so on.

The CEO must become aware of the existence and power of these forces upon the members and, therefore, of the necessity to ensure uniformity of approach. Members are pulled in different directions at the same time and need help with the focus and alignment.

A fifth problem is not unique to top teams but can be very destructive and it refers to the *ambiguity in roles*. Executive team members are answerable to many different constituencies. More importantly it is not always clear how decisions are made. Executives need to specify very clearly *how* the group is to make decisions and, of necessity, to stick to them.

Decision making is at the essence of the board's duty. And decision making involves a pretty clearly followed process. This concerns things such as a goal analysis, a decision about how to decide (individuals versus groups, use of experts), the generation of alternatives, the choosing of alternatives, and so on. Some decisions are relatively minor and may be made by the chairperson or indeed specialist board experts. Others need to be considered by everybody. But it is important to know what type of decisions require what sort of response by whom, and by when.

The sixth problem is the personal, but not *hidden agendas of individuals*. The boardroom is an ideal place, some believe, to have fun, to promote personal causes; they ride hobby horses. To have important and powerful people pay attention to one's personal issues is too attractive an opportunity to miss for some directors whose politico-religious or other crypto-philosophical agendas can highjack board meetings for hours.

The solution is quite simple: have a clear agenda and stick to it. Boards need to be told on a regular basis what they are there for.

It is too easy to see the problems of the board in terms of the lack of ability or simply the pathology of the individual members. Some directors do make it to board level with remarkably mediocre ability. Others have exploited their personal pathology (narcissism or paranoia) to rise in the organisation. But hopefully they remain the minority; though in some companies this is far from clear.

It is the role of the chairperson to get the best out of the board through optimal membership, appropriate control and openness; getting members focused and clear about their role and joint agenda is not easy with self-important grown-ups, but it is essential to ensure board functioning.

Psychologists in business

Few people in business either have, or will admit to having met a psychologist, lest others imagine they are in, or need, therapy. That is, unless the psychologist happens to be an executive coach, which is somehow OK. Most people are unable to distinguish between a psychologist, psychoanalyst, psychiatrist and a psychiatric social worker.

Actually it is easy: a psychologist is a person who goes to a strip show but looks at the audience; a psychoanalyst teaches people how to stand on their own two feet by lying them down on a couch for years; a psychiatrist is a doctor who is afraid of the sight of blood; a psychiatric social worker makes you feel better but encourages you to blame all your problems on your parents.

But there is a new breed stalking the land: the organisational psychologist, even the grandly termed Chartered Organisational Psychologist. Who are these 'ologists'? What can they offer? How are they different from the average management consultant?

To become a chartered organisational psychologist, which can take two to three years after an appropriately recognised masters degree, one has to prove expertise in eight areas of business life. These are:

1. Human machine interaction.
2. Design of environments and work: health and safety
3. Personnel selection and assessment, including test and exercise design
4. Performance appraisal and career development
5. Counselling and personal development
6. Training (identification of needs, training design and evaluation).
7. Employee relations and motivation
8. Organisational development and change.

Most people erroneously believe that all psychologists are 'insightful', 'emotionally intelligent', 'good with people'. The stereotypic psychologist has some sort of miraculous and privileged understanding of human personality, motives and abilities. This is simply wrong. Not even clinicians or psychotherapists fall into this category. Some are good at it. But don't expect it.

So what is special about psychologists? Psychologists tend to be good at behavioural measurement. They really should know about psychometrics. They use different data bases: self-report interviews, questionnaires, tests and should have a good knowledge of statistical analysis.

They should also have a sophisticated language to describe individual differences. Psychologists should be able not only to describe individual differences but *explain* them. They should be able also to describe the psychological processes that differentiate people. It's easy to categorise – much harder and more important to explain the mechanisms and processes.

Many psychologists have knowledge and expertise in individual differences. Differences in issues of preference: beliefs, interests, values and traits and issues of abilities, namely intelligence. Alas some greedy, pragmatic consultants and test-publishers without suitable qualifications or up-to-date knowledge have oversold tests to hungry but naive purchasers. Such mis-selling has given all psychometrics a bad name.

Psychologists should also be good at diagnosis. Diagnosis precedes cure and it is often harder than cure. Everyone in business knows that many business problems – absenteeism, accidents, customer complaints, unacceptable staff turnover – are often behavioural manifestations of other problems. The problem as presented by management for fixing is frequently not the real issue. Psychologists should be good at understanding the cause and consequence of behavioural problems, be it bullying, work over- or underloading or role ambiguity.

Psychologists should know a thing or two about training. After all, educational psychologists for over 100 years have been trying to understand optimal training methods. Consider, for instance, the well-known issue of massed versus distributed learning. If you have a three-day course, should you run it on a Monday, Tuesday and Wednesday or three consecutive Mondays? The answer is the latter. Psychologists should be able to measure the efficacy of training.

They should, if it's their specialism, know about ergonomics, task/ work designs and new technology. Others should have a reasonable grasp of legal issues such as equal opportunities or health and safety. The crypto or quasi clinical types often favour guidance and counselling roles along with stress management and career development.

Inevitably, occupational psychologists have their own profiles of expertise and preferences. They all have their own strengths and developmental opportunities. And, like all experts and consultants, the good ones can add a great deal to organisational insight, efficiency and productivity, while the less talented only add to the overheads.

Psychology of hoarding

Remember the paperless office? One of the many unfulfilled promises of the web was that the snail mail would die along with all that expensively produced and desperately unecological paper. Indeed the web seems to lead to more rather than less paper for many business people.

Paperlessness was not to be and business people daily have to fight the battle of the paper mountain. The internal and external mail, let alone what one prints from the web and emails, arrives at an alarming rate. It would not be unusual to receive between 50 and 200 paper messages a week, from flyers to minutes of the meeting. But what to do with all that paper?

People interested in these sorts of things have distinguished between healthy and unhealthy responses to the influx of paper. The healthy response is supposedly *file, act or toss*, while the unhealthy response is supposedly *pile, copy and store*.

What the gurus say is first examine the document. Is it important? Will you need reference to it? If so file it in a way it is easily retrievable. If you don't need to keep a copy but simply act on what it demands, suggests or recommends, just do it. Now! Then throw it away. Finally, a good deal of what you get simply requires losing – immediately. Bureaucracy, bumf and balderdash need swift binning, even shredding.

Of course, the unhealthy responses are first to pile incoming paper on the desk. You still see the cartoons with people with piles of papers in trays labelled IN or OUT. Some are labelled TOO DIFFICULT and others THROUGH-PUT. People pile because they believe they do not have the time to read the material and make a decision on it at the speed it arrives. So they pile it until they can get 'around to it'. Pile grows: things get lost; the urgent and trivial are not separated. And people become simply overwhelmed.

Worse still, certain papers are copied, cc'd and redistributed to increase the paper mountain; the urge to copy is a main factor in the problem. But so is the urge to store which is very different from the act to file. Storing is about hoarding; filing is about classifying.

At the simplest level the whole paper problem is about the psychology of hoarding. Hoarding appears to be a powerful instinct: many animals do it for their very survival. But there is a difference between hoarding and storing.

Pathological hoarding has been associated with an obsessive/compulsive personality syndrome. Hoarders, according to the theory, are likely to be very concerned with cleanliness, time-keeping and order.

The Freudians argue that these attitudes start very early: in fact at the potty training age. Further difficulties at this time can lead to opposite behaviours – both rather abnormal. Thus the obsessional hoarder and miser as well as the compulsive spendthrift may have had a traumatic power-conflict over the potty.

Freud identified three main traits associated with people who had fixated at the anal stage: orderliness, parsimony and obstinacy with associated qualities of cleanliness, conscientiousness, trustworthiness, defiance and revengefulness.

The Freudian aetiology of hoarding theory goes something like this:

The child's first interest in his faeces turns first to such things as mud, sand, stones, thence to all man-made objects that can be collected (like paper), and thence to money. Children all experience pleasure in the elimination of faeces. At an early age (around 2 years) parents toilet train their children – some showing enthusiasm and praise (positive reinforcement) for defecation, others threatening and punishing a child when it refuses to do so (negative reinforcement). Potty or toilet training occurs at the same stage that the child is striving to achieve autonomy and a sense of worth. Often toilet training becomes a source of conflict between parents and children over whether the child is in control of his sphincter or whether the parental rewards and coercion compel submission to their will. Furthermore the child is fascinated by and fantasises over his faeces which are, after all, a creation of his own body. The child's confusion is made all the worse by the ambiguous reactions of parents who on the one hand treat the faeces as gifts and highly valued, and then behave as if they are dirty, untouchable and in need of immediate disposal.

If the child is traumatised by the experience of toilet training, he tends to retain ways of coping and behaving during this phase. The way in which a miser hoards money and paper is symbolic of the child's refusal to eliminate faeces in the face of parental demands. The spendthrift, on the other hand, recalls the approval and affection that resulted from submission to parental authority to defecate. Thus some people equate elimination/spending with receiving affection and hence felt more inclined to spend when feeling insecure, unloved or in need of affection. Attitudes to money and hoarding are then bimodal – either they are extremely positive or extremely negative.

Families, groups and societies which demand early and rigid toilet training tend to produce 'anal characteristics' in people, which include hoarding, orderliness, punctuality, compulsive cleanliness and obstinacy. Hence one can be miserly about informational time and emotions as much as money. These effects may be increased or reduced depending on whether the child grows up in a socialist or capitalist country, in times of comparative expansion or depression, or whether one is part of a middle- or working-class family. Parents' belief in the Puritan or Protestant ethic may also alter money beliefs and habits.

It is merely embarrassing nonsense all this Freudian stuff? If so, one does have to explain the almost pathological hoarding that some people get up to. They know it is unhealthy and inefficient. They know the file, act, toss mantra is sensible. They often feel however pretty powerless to do otherwise unless they get help. Hence the consultants who offer a mixture of bullying and psychotherapy seem best at helping the pathological hoarder – as well as the merely disorganised.

Selection mistakes

Selecting people is a serious business. Despite the efforts of both trainers and therapists adults are pretty hard to change. The package of abilities, attitudes and traits found in a person in their mid-twenties will probably quite happily (or alas unhappily) see them through to the grave.

Brides who think 'I'll alter him' rather than 'Aisle, Altar, Hymn' are frequently bitterly disappointed. Our divorce statistics are testament to poor selection decisions.

Selection is at least, in principle, a straightforward process. Select the good; reject the bad. The problem is the other two groups. We learn from only one source of error; selecting the bad; we never know about the good we have rejected.

When a person or an organisation has made a seriously bad decision, they sometimes, but not often enough, go back to the files, to try to see where they made an error. What data/information did they not collect? How did they interpret something incorrectly? Who did they not talk to who could have helped them?

Poor selection decisions cost a great deal. And they can, in part, be prevented by doing three things. The first error is to think one is exclusively in the select-in, rather than the *select-out business*. Traditionally, what selectors do is list the attributes they want in the person. These are frequently called competencies which helps explain the problem because their origins are never defined. Are competencies abilities or traits? Are they changeable, and if so, how?

Most selectors have pet theories about the process. Most have an idea that certain characteristics are bad news. Evidence of a prison record may convince selectors not to give the person a second chance. These select-out factors usually apply more to errors of omission than commission, that is, things that should have been done that weren't, as opposed to things that were done that, in their judgement, were a mistake.

But what abilities or traits might serve as select-out factors? We know from recent reviews of hundreds of studies on thousands of people that there are three important predictors of success at work, however measured. One is the ability factor, namely general intelligence; the other two are traits, namely emotional stability (the opposite of neuroticism) and conscientiousness or the work ethic. Successful people have to be bright enough, stable, hard workers. If they are dim, neurotic and lazy they fail.

So these characteristics should serve as select-out criteria. We need evidence that a person is *bright enough* to do the job. Bright people have more confidence, learn faster, adapt to change better. People who are emotionally stable can cope with stress better; they can support others more effectively. The work ethic is associated with perseverance, prudence and dutifulness.

But perhaps neuroticism is the most important select-out factor. Some jobs already do this: bomb disposal personnel, submariners, fire-fighters, airplane pilots all have to be stable in the face of stress. And they are rigorously screened for their emotional stability. But what about executives?

Many a talented 'wunderkind' has derailed under the impact of stress. Psychologists talk of hardiness, which is a good concept expressing what one searches for in employees. But the question remains: does the select-out process actively and explicitly seek for evidence of hardiness and stability? Neuroticism is a select-out variable. It is a robust predictor of failure. It should be, but is not, a central feature in any selection process. Perhaps it is too embarrassing or selectors do not feel confident enough to tackle it, ignoring or downplaying it, and other select-out factors.

The second mistake is the assumption of linearity. What that means is that selectors believe there is a linear relationship between a competency and any job performance. In other words: the more the merrier. Thus if creativity or innovativeness are thought of as important competencies then selectors believe the more one has of this quality the better one does in the job.

There are a number of possible relationships between a competence and performance. First, it would be linear: more competency better performance. Second, there could be a cut-off point, meaning that once a level of competency has been reached there is no noticeable increase in performance. Third, that it could be an inverse U shaped curve suggesting, perhaps paradoxically to some, that one can have too much of a good thing.

Can one be too bright, too creative, too conscientious for a job? The answer is yes. They very bright can be prone to boredom or analysis paralysis. The very creative are often very impractical and terribly difficult to manage. The very conscientious may turn into workaholics, never understanding the idea of work smart is work hard or the difference between presentism or productivity.

Having great strengths is, of course, most desirable, but they may hide weaknesses. Just as being too tall or too short can be problematic in many jobs so having too much or too little of any competency can lead to failure.

The trick therefore is to specify, measure and select those at the optimum level. This is by no means easy but it is important. Selectors are certainly used to the concept of 'too little'. They are much less familiar with the idea of 'too much'.

The third selection mistake is to rely on one source of data. Whether it is an application form or face-to-face interview, most selection involves getting applicants to talk about themselves. But all interviewees and a substantial number of interviewers, are in the business of impression management. Some people cannot, rather than will not, talk about their motives and experiences through lack of insight.

So interviewers try another source of data: observational data by calling for references. But they nearly all do so from the wrong people namely those who have been in authority over the interviewees such as their previous boss or teacher.

Those in the 360-degree feedback business know that four groups of 'observers' can comment on an individual's performance: boss, peers, subordinates, customers. Each of these groups has different experiences of, and data on, the individual. Who knows the person best? Who has the richest and most subtle database? Answer: subordinates. They know all about their manager precisely because they 'suffer' most the consequences of his/her style. They really know whether the manager understands accounts, computers, and the like; they know when he or she has a hangover or is going shopping; they know they don't get real appraisals.

If subordinate reports are the best informed about an applicant's abilities and traits they, not the manager should be asked. And asked in detail about all aspects of performance. There is often quite a number of them which is good for a reliable response. Guaranteed anonymity, they are perhaps the best source of data on any applicant.

The moral of the story is this. To reduce selection errors have select-out, as well as select-in criteria. Consider how much each desirable attribute/ competency is required; and get the applicants' reports/subordinates to provide reference data, not only their bosses.

Selling cost-saving devices

Answer three simple (Yes/No) questions (i) Would you prefer a 'closed plan' office of your own to working in an open-planned office arrangement? (ii) Would you prefer learning/training with a 'live' lecturer or trainer at work to being taught by e-learning methods? (iii) Would you prefer to interview, negotiate or conference a person in another country face-to-face to going through a video-link-up facility?

By far the majority of answers to these questions is a resounding yes. Why then do we read so much from managers and trainers, architects and accountants, consultants and auditors about the benefits of open-plan, e-learning and video-conferencing. The answer is simple: *cost.*

People who resist the changes to the new working style are labelled old-fashioned, change-averse; even worse 'trouble makers'. Retention as well as promotion may be dependent on accepting these changes. Irrespective of the research on this topic.

Consider the open-planned office. Proponents, who appreciate all the cost savings associated with this move, talk about facilitating communication, breaking down barriers and improving teamwork. They say little about productivity, problems of confidentiality and general distractibility.

There are good reasons to resist open-planned offices. Introverts are particularly unhappy in these environments, nearly always proposed by garrulous extraverts who enjoy the adrenalin buzz of open plan. Introverts are more easily disturbed by noises and interruptions than extraverts. They are exhausted by frequent interruptions and their productivity drops.

Open plan is bad for complex tasks involving considerable concentration. Consider the classic exam room which is, of course, open plan to ensure both economy and ease of observation. Silence is very strictly enforced because examinees can't think with noise. But you can't enforce silence in open plan: alas productivity in complex tasks declines.

Professionals need privacy. Conversations about clients' issues sometimes need to be completely confidential. While it is possible to have these in open-planned offices, it is not always easy. And if clients know the open-planned arrangement, they may not disclose in the first place.

Nearly always the mockery of the ever taller, thicker, sound-proofed barriers erected in the open-planned office shows how desperate people are to be closed planned. Perhaps it's a basic animal instinct fulfilling primitive Maslowian needs for safety and security.

But a move to open-planned is good for the bottom-line: it means more people in a smaller more adaptable space. The workplace of the new millennium is becoming as unnatural and unpleasant as those typing-pool rooms of 100 years ago.

And note that when organisations go open plan just a few manage to retain their old, private, closed space in the office. They are always the 'top dogs'. Try finding out the rationale of these exceptions: the question may be desperately career-limiting but it is instructive of the real reasons behind open plan.

And what about e-learning? Just as space is expensive so are people. Teachers, trainers and instructors are very expensive as are training facilities. So why not replace them with a diskette. Employees are told there are many benefits to e-learning whether it is 'live' or not: you can do the work at any time that suits you; and at any place (if you have a laptop). You can go at your speed and contact other students (and they you) when you feel like it. You may even be able to contact a tutor.

Any student of the Open University knows the benefits and drawbacks of distance learning whether or not it is electronic. And they know the importance, as well as the delight, of those weekends where you meet face-to-face your fellow students and lecturers. It's the conversation over meals about what one does or does not understand; practising arguing skills after too much red wine and getting a comparative sense of·how good you are, that are important.

The electronic medium might be quick but it's cold, impersonal and liable to be scrutinised by others. Of course it is no doubt true that some topics may be happily and efficiently learnt through an e-based programme. But this does tend to differ from individual to individual and on their abilities, learning style and educational backgrounds. Some tasks and topics just don't seem suited to the web.

And what about video-conferencing? In fact these sorts of facilities have been around for over 30 years but never proved as popular as manufacturers and pundits hoped. Sure it saves on travel time and money, which can be considerable. But the medium does tend to pro and prescribe behaviour. People tend to 'get on with it' much more quickly. This is particularly problematic with bargaining or negotiation where timing is often of the essence.

The experience of 'being there' is known to sports fans. It is cheaper to watch on the TV at home, often with better views (and all that slow-motion repeat stuff). But this is a poor substitute for the smell of the turf and the roar of the crowd.

But is this just a matter of getting used to new conditions and new media? What you have never had you never miss? Partly; but it is also about fundamentally understanding people. We are social animals designed for interaction and learning in a particular way. Yet we all need our own space in which to feel confident and safe.

Many changes at work are not driven by ergonomic ingenuity or psychological analysis. They are driven by economic necessity – or sometimes greedy shareholders. And it is organisational spin doctors who have to try to cover up the real reasons for the changes by presenting a positive, highly biased, picture of the benefits of the new way.

Sociobiology and inheritance tax

Some of the most successful popular books over the past 30 years have been based on evolutionary theory. Whether they have to do with altruism (*The Selfish Gene*) or relationships (*Men are from Mars, Women are from Venus*) or general behaviour (*Man Watching*), they all endorse a neo-Darwinian view of human nature. Evolutionary theorists and their more zealous sociobiological cousins have powerful, intriguing and sometimes counter-intuitive explanations for all sorts of behaviours. Early work focused on topics such as cooperation, reciprocity and sharing. More recent work has dwelled on mate choice and selection.

As ever, certain ideas have caught the public imagination. Consider mate selection: put crudely, we select mates that help our genes survive. What women want in men is intelligence (good sense of humour), health (six-pack, tight bottom) and wealth (good job). They want a man to give them healthy, bright babies, which he is in a position to look after. Men on the other hand want women who are fecund. And one of the best indications of that is her hip-to-waist ratio. Medium sized, curvy, seductive (but faithful) women is what all men want.

Some studies have investigated what are called parental investment decisions. They have also looked at such issues as how people draw up their wills and how they make decisions about what to leave to whom.

Why do parents scrimp and save and become seriously self-denying to send their children to private schools, and why is inheritance tax such a hot topic? Because these actions are in fact hard-wired survival strategies that are being tampered with by politicians. Draconian inheritance tax is powerfully unnatural in the sense that it seems to be anti-Darwinian.

The Chancellor made £2.4 billion from inheritance tax in the United Kingdom two years ago. Left-wing politicians want a more democratic society and hence favour increasing inheritance tax. Right-wingers want to abolish it to encourage parents in their natural and healthy desire to help their children as much as possible.

While there are cultural differences in practice there is clear evidence that the distribution of wealth to descendants operates as evolutionary theory would predict. Parental investment of time, money and protection in their offspring is a very powerful desire.

All parents want the best for their children. They all say the same regarding their hopes for children: all they want is for them to be happy and healthy. And they also know that while money might not guarantee either, it certainly can help prevent their opposites: unhappiness and illness.

But all parents, and rich(er) parents in particular, know that if their children are to use rather than abuse their inheritance, they have to understand money. Many self-made parents lavish money on their children, who then proceed to squander it, so that, as the cynic remarked, the family moves from the 'gutter to the gutter in one generation'.

Other parents are very strict, even mean with their children, to try to teach them the real value of money. This may mean tying up money in a complicated trust that parents hope/insist/require is spent wisely. More likely, however, it will involve teaching children about saving and spending, tax and investments.

Because of the rise of property prices in particular, but wealth in general over the past 20 years, middle-middle and lower-middle class parents are beginning to find that they have enough money to be liable to inheritance tax. It comes as quite a shock. The rich, particularly those with old money, have had plans in place for years to, shall we say, reduce these taxes through avoidance measures.

Yet, quite suddenly, the hard-working, self-sacrificing parent is being confronted by something that seems both 'unfair and unnatural'. The deep-seated, biologically based drive to help protect and succour one's offspring seems challenged by an alien, social-engineering dogma, that punishes the fit. No wonder the uncontrollable rage on the topic as manifest by letters to the editor.

Strategic planning: who needs it?

Is a company's success inversely related to its number of strategic planners? Has strategic planning lost its shine? The eighties were the heyday of these number-tumbling wonderkids, freshly minted from business school. But where are they now?

Strategy wasn't an option, it was a necessity, we were told. You needed a long-term plan for growth, restructuring, even survival. You needed to look for trends; realistically evaluate what you had got and what it was worth before acting. Tactics were for managers, strategy for leaders. If you wanted to get ahead, you got a strategy department; had a place on the board for someone of director level; took it seriously.

But was that all hype? Was the money well spent on in-house strategy johnnies as well as those charge-like-a wounded-bull consultants? Or was it like the dot.com boom or millennium bug IT scare?

The problems of strategic planning are essentially threefold: futurology is a (very) inexact science; who owns and implements the strategy in strategic planning; and how inflexible it is.

The first issue is that of forecasting. Edmund Burke wisely noted that you can (and therefore should) never plan the future by the past. Many forecasters have got it wrong, including some pretty clever scientists. Consider the following:

- 'I think there is a world market for maybe five computers.' *Thomas Watson, Chairman of IBM, 1943*
- 'Space travel is utter bilge.' *Richard Riet Woolley, British Astronomer Royal, 1956*
- 'There is no reason for any individuals to have a computer in their home.' *Ken Olsen, President and Founder of Digital Equipment Corporation, 1977*
- 'This telephone has too many shortcomings … as a means of communication … the device is inherently of no value.' *Western Union internal memo, 1876*
- 'The light bulb … unworthy of the attention of practical or scientific men.' *British Parliamentary Committee, 1883*

■ 'Heavier than air flying machines are impossible.' *Lord Kelvin, President, The Royal Society, 1895*

Less than 10 years ago the futurologists thought we now would have:

■ The paperless office
■ 20-hour week
■ Flights: London–LA in 1 hour
■ Astronaut food
■ Russian hegemony.

And we are told by these breathless followers of fashion that the new world will be so different from the last:

Old World	*New World*
■ Wired	■ Wireless
■ Office Hours	■ 24/7
■ Corporate Headquarters	■ Centres-Companies
■ Local/Global Markets	■ Web-based Marketing
■ e-excitement	■ e-fatigue
■ Surplus of Youth	■ Surplus of Wrinklies

Futurologists tell us that there will be no more jobs for life. There will be a change of emphasis from being employed to being employable. Job security will be based on performance and therefore individuals need to take responsibility for their own learning. Greater global competition will lead to greater speed of reaction, reducing product life cycles and increasing focus on core business and delivery. And there will be a continuing reduction of the permanent workforce: already 41% of today's workforce is temporary or (short-term) contract.

And these characters do like the c-word. Tomorrow will see all sorts of changes:

■ Changes in the *workforce* in terms of cultural diversity, skill, experience and expectations, which probably differ significantly from one country to another.
■ Changes in *customer expectations*, which normally means a rise in the quality and reliability of products, and the excellence of service demanded.

■ Changes in the *size, structure and international focus* and the managers needed to run them. Economic, legal, social and competitive forces mean that companies have to adapt, reinvent themselves, and re-engineer simply to survive, let alone prosper.

■ Changes in *economic conditions* governed by new inventions (the electronic revolution), raw material (the exhaustion of certain assets), and political cooperation and competition.

The trick is to evaluate changes in the economic world and respond to them while there is time!

The problem with forecasting is simple: the further ahead and more important it is, the less accurate. Most strategic planners see the plan as five years or more, just when forecasts change into speculation, guesswork and wobbly extrapolation.

There is one other dangerous feature of most organisations' strategic plans: *naive optimism*. The plan is about what will and should happen and is a best guess of what to do to ensure not just success but for the entity to thrive. So the plan nearly always paints a picture of increased profitability, growth and the like. Remember the dot.com hype and a vision of the (near) future which did not materialise.

The second major issue for the strategic plan is ownership and implementation. Two somewhat opposite models in fact share the same problem. If a company has a strategic planning department made up of smart young things, they are able to produce very impressive reports and presentations. They gather the data, plot the graphs, tumble the numbers, decide on the logical actions and then usually give the report to the CEO. The question is, what then happens? If the boss understands it and then approves it, then what? He or they then present it to the directors, who are of course very directly involved. Do they understand it and approve it?

We all know that the major function of business meetings has nothing to do with enhancing the quality of decision making – it's about having buy-in. To be given a plan conceived by others that very crucially involves your department is not likely to encourage much enthusiastic participation. Even if they have been 'consulted' (even extensively so) the grown-ups resent being handed a complex strategy dictated from above. So they argue, resist implementation and the impressive-looking grand plan collects dust.

The other model for creation of a plan is bottom-up, rather than top-down. It is collectivist, home-grown and devised by non-experts. So, with some help, the top team develops its own detailed strategy. The question is, who coordinates this activity, which takes time and diplomacy? Data have to be gathered, ideas elicited and powerfully opposing camps reconciled. Some CEOs can perform this role but most cannot. So a facilitator has to be appointed who has to coordinate, compromise and coerce the participants.

The bottom-up approach takes a good deal more investment of time than the top-down diktat – time the organisation may not have the luxury of in deciding its next move. Especially if the banks and competitors are circling an enterprise in trouble …

A bottom-up plan can be a dog's breakfast of a thing that is neither clear nor logical but reflects the political skill or bullying of the various players. But still the issue remains: who is ultimately responsible for the total, cost-effective and timely implementation of the plan? Too difficult, so not done! All the plans have three phrases in which time and money need to be invested: devising the plan, implementing it and maintaining the changes. Often, so much energy is spent on the first phase that there is nothing left for subsequent phases.

The third problem lies in the flexibility of plans. Plans involve trend forecasting and business estimates. It is not unusual for market or world events to occur very suddenly and majorly impact on business. Imagine what SARS and 9/11 did to airline plans. The issue is how easy it is to recalibrate a trajectory and indeed recalculate the forecasts. It is a bad plan that admits no modification. Many strategic plans have an all-or-nothing feel about them. A lot of effort was put into the calculations, the market segmentation, the cost analysis and so on. So much so that one dare not tinker. And yet a completely new plan is necessary.

So do you need a plan? Naturally. Do you need planners? Not necessarily. Better have a flexible, short-termish plan that is agreed and owned by the implementers. Not an easy achievement – but worth planning for.

Support groups for CEOs

It is not only the long-distance runner or the commercial traveller who are lonely in their jobs. They spend long periods of time alone which is certainly a hardship for the latter group, who are usually very social animals.

CEOs also report loneliness which is paradoxical given they spend long periods with people. All day long they chair meetings, open (but not close) plants, press the flesh, talk at conferences and counsel directors reporting to them. Despite all this contact they complain about being lonely. What they mean is that they are required to play a variety of roles rather than be themselves. They have always to be diplomatic, guarded, confident and reassuring.

The question is who the CEO turns to when he/she is worried, depressed, uncertain, troubled and the like. Often CEOs, like the Almighty, are required to be omniscient, omni-present and omnipotent. So in the midst of others they have to remain confident and up-beat, no matter how they feel.

So what do the CEOs do if they feel lonely at the top? Some use their long-suffering spouse as a sounding board, a shoulder to cry on – and also an outlet for their frustrations. Others might find a hobby/pastime with people quite different from themselves where they either sublimate their frustration with balls, rackets, fast cars ... even fast women. At these hobby-based events they may find a confidant to whom they can talk about their worries. This can be very helpful in fulfilling a powerful human need.

The CEO seeking an out-of-business confidant is almost the precise opposite of the posh middle-aged woman having a bit-of-rough for a rumpy pumpy affair. She wants a simple physical relationship. Our CEO, is by definition, a complex beast who wants to talk.

The modern CEO has three options: a friend, a coach, a social support group. Friends are free but hard to find. Ideally they need to be good listeners, perspicacious, wise, with business savvy and empathy. They need to be utterly trustworthy, stable and easily contactable. But where to find them? And what's in it for them? Perhaps an old school friend? It is hard enough finding new friends when middle aged. Even harder to find a supportive, caring, insightful sounding board.

Currently the fad is for a coach. The precise role of the business coach remains unclear: part therapist, part academic, part guru. Is a coach anything more than a paid friend? And where do you find and select them? It's a new 'profession' but judging from their growth in numbers and often frankly unbelievable hourly rates they are certainly fulfilling some important need.

It may be fashionable, even a status symbol to have a coach these days. This in itself attests to the needs of the lonely CEO in need of support, good council and advice.

The trouble with coaches is finding the right one. One wants a coach with relevant business experience, self-insight, and training in coaching. They need at best to have a theoretical approach, a framework and some idea of what success and failure look like. But even more they need to look, sound and smell right to both parties. CEOs can have beauty parades in an attempt to select the right person but this can be a seriously hit-or-miss affair. Often they get recommendations from colleagues but, as we all discover at dinner parties, even close friends are not necessarily to one's tastes.

There is a third option and one that has being going for a long time: the social support group. They come in a variety of guises, call themselves different names, but they function to provide an excellent forum for advice contacts as support. The Buffalos, Legions, Masons and Rotarians have been around for a long time. They have different but overlapping missions but look at their membership and go to their meetings to see why their members are there. Now we have other versions. Some call themselves FORA, others are more open like TEC who bill themselves as the organisation of CEOs.

In these clubs, societies and groups one can find like-minded people with like-minded problems. CEOs with different businesses, of different sizes and structures and in quite different sectors still have similar problems. How best to lay off staff; how to deal with untrustworthy suppliers; how much to spend on advertising.

The CEO (or even the COs, CFOs) in these groups can learn a great deal as they hear different solutions to similar problems. Having guest speakers every so often may also help as they provoke excellent debates.

In these groups the CEO can unwind and unburden him/herself especially as many either openly or tacitly acknowledge Chatham House rules. Some are thus even prepared to take out a day a month to attend these events that bring them tremendous personal and business benefit.

Teaching old dogs new tricks

The L-word is spreading. People with a particular *learning style* work in *action learning groups* in a *learning organisation*. They are encouraged, to indulge in *life long learning*, perhaps *e-learning* after a *learning needs analysis*. But what needs to be learnt, by whom, and when is not always clear. What is clear to any training manager is that the world is neatly divided into learno-phobes and learno-philes. The former strongly resist all learning initiatives, the latter embrace them all.

Naturally attention is focused on the non-believers and non-combatants. Who are they and why do they resist? Old dogs, senior people and the uncommitted make up many of the opt-out, won't play, non learners – or at least those who don't want to be taught.

There are two antonymous proverbs of relevance here: ' you are never too old to learn', and quite contrary, 'you can't teach an old dog new tricks'. Which is true? Does this explain why people resist and seem unwilling to learn? Is it only a matter of age?

There are three sorts of factors, which appear to predict willingness to take part in learning. Two are pretty immutable and they affect the third which fortunately is. The first factor is our learning history specifically our experience of secondary school and beyond. Experience of exam success and failure has shaped expectations of the learning process: how easy/difficult it is; how much fun it all is; and the cost–benefit analysis.

To a large extent these expectations are shaped by the whole business of social comparison. This means how well a person has done compared (as he/she sees it) to their peers. Thus the peer group is fundamentally important to the whole business. At school and university people get a sense of their ability, their preferred learning style and how good they are at learning new things.

Over the years, adults develop a series of ever-more elaborate stories justifying their lack of success in educational contexts. Poor teaching, undiagnosed cognitive problems, poor facilities, various types of discrimination all feature highly. On the other hand, learning success can neatly and succinctly be attributed to ability, with a little effort.

Adults at work have strong memories of learning contexts. They have clear beliefs about how right they are; what is easy to learn and what's not. And, not unnaturally, they will strongly resist being 'shown up' or having to endure tedious and difficult tasks that bring little obvious benefit.

The past is a different country. It is done. But memories can be changed and they influence strongly how people approach any new learning. Clearly good experiences in the past predict willingness (also probably) ability to do so in the future.

The second set of factors refers to a person's actual intelligence and personality. Bright people learn faster; they are able to learn more complicated things. Amen. People need to be bright enough to learn whatever is being taught. It is harder to learn Mandarin than Spanish. Bright people, particularly those with a good ear, do better.

The question then is roughly what level of intelligence should be the 'cut-off' point for each learning exercise. And related to this is 'do people have a realistic view of their own intelligence?' Most do, but because of inaccurate feedback there are the problems of hubris and humility: the less bright who think they are, and the talented who seem unsure of their ability. Testing people thoroughly and giving them accurate, honest feedback on their performance should overcome the problem.

Three personality variables are clearly implicated in the whole learning business: conscientiousness, neuroticism and openness to experience. Conscientiousness or whatever synonym one prefers – diligence, the work ethic, achievement striving, prudence – are all good predictors of learning success. The conscientious work harder, longer and smarter. They take learning seriously. They put in extra effort and are usually suitably rewarded. Neuroticism, on the other hand, is a poor predictor of learning willingness and success. Neurotics are anxious and easily depressed by setbacks. They worry a lot. And their anxiety is often self-handicapping. They tend to be more tense, and more prone to illness (real or imagined) and tend to go absent more. A moderate amount of worry may be good news as it may motivate people to try harder. But go above this level and one has known learning problems.

Openness to experience is about willingness to try something new, particularly to explore new ideas, emotions and experiences. It is about curiosity and creativity. It's more than a 'have-a-go mentality'. It's partly about exploration and the joy of the new. It's a good predictor of both ability and willingness to learn.

So to have bright, conscientious, open and stable people in the organisation bodes well. But there is something else which is influenced by all of the above factors. And that is *self-esteem* or *self-belief*. It's about confidence in one's ability and not being afraid to be seen as in need of help.

Indeed the reason senior executives often eschew training courses is not about time (the favoured excuse) or even cost–benefit analysis. It is the fear of being 'shown-up' as less able and knowledgeable than they like to pretend. They are usually much happier to do one-on-one learning because it is private. Hence the popularities of coaching which is often a mixture of counselling and teaching.

All clinicians will tell you that self-esteem is difficult but possible to budge. They will also tell you that it often bares little relation to reality. Just as anorexic patients see themselves as obese so some talented, able people see themselves as 'pretty average'. And vice versa – but these over confident, even arrogant types are another story.

The good trainer knows that adults are nervous about learning. Particularly older people who probably did not have the educational opportunities of the young and who feel, often quite correctly, that their memory and cognitive agility is not what is used to be. The good trainer gives hesitant adult learners early experience of success, without patronising them. And shows them the benefit, and yes even joy, of learning something new that is both interesting and useful.

Telling clients what they want to hear

All salesmen know the dilemma well: should you tell clients what they want to hear, or the mundane, far less attractive, truth? Only point out strengths and ignore weaknesses? For some it pricks the conscience. But business people and consultants know their lives are easier, happier and richer if they simply give in and agree with the clients and do what they want, irrespective of whether their decisions are wise or not.

The issue, at least in HR, can be ever more complicated. The business press and management literature are awash with inspirational stories of how people turned around a workforce, made millions, or transformed a whole industry by the introduction of some simple technique or other.

And there are also words of wisdom handed down about psychological phenomena relevant to business. Some are true … ish, others completely wrong. Sometimes there is an absence of evidence, other times evidence of absence of the effect.

Consider the dilemma faced by a management consultant in challenging times. The clients want a training programme which they believe will turn round their poor revenue growth. The clients have read about this 'miraculous cure' in a business magazine. The consultant knows that this is all flimflam and that the 'cure' must be quite different. The clients are insistent and have the money to spend on the programme which the consultant is able to deliver. Is there an ethical issue here, or is the customer king? The customer may be right, or simply naive. Wise consultants, protective of their business reputations would probably walk away from a situation if they feel they cannot guarantee good results. Others may be willing to take a gamble …

Consider the following five customer ideas:

1. *Creativity can be taught*
Really creative individuals are both rare and difficult to manage. Most of us like to believe we are creative and that, whatever our base level of creativity, we can get better – more creative, more innovative, more zany. But the evidence is against us. You can learn a few 'tricks', but creative genius takes a particular combination of effort and, especially, innate ability. It is as much about perspiration as inspiration. Study the lives of the creative

for the evidence. Courses called 'Unblocking your creative talent' only unblock your wallet.

2. *First impressions count most*
Experts in the PR and fashion business like to say that people in inter-views (and so on) 'make up their mind' in the first three minutes or so. The idea is that information – often visual, impressionistic – that comes first is more important than that which comes last. Psychologists call this the primacy-recency effect. And good experimental data show that often recency information (that which comes last) has more impact. Ask any lawyer whether he wants the first or last word to the jury.

First impressions count; but they can change. Poor vocabulary over-powers the first impression of education based on clothes. Negative infor-mation soon cancels positive information whenever it is presented. Beware impression management consultants; they have not done their homework. After three minutes they may seem more like charlatans.

3. *Non-verbal information is more important/powerful than verbal information*
Oh, yes … have you ever tried playing charades, where all that is available is non-verbal communication (NVC)? Talk to world experts on lying and they tell you it is difficult accurately to detect dissimilation in adults. Most people have little enough insight into their own emotions and motives, let alone those of others. NVC experts quote bogus figures, such as that 75 per cent of what we convey is done non-verbally. They don't know where that figure comes from: actually a poorly done study in the late 1960s. They also love the idea that all non-verbal behaviour is symbolic of deeply seated Freudian wishes, for which there is no evidence. Sure, being non-verbally aware is a good thing. Sensitivity to cues can be learnt but they are not the x-ray vision some imply. Listen carefully to what people say. Psychologists and Catholic priests interact via couches and confessionals which prevent the possibility of NVC. And they should know.

4. *EQ can be easily learnt*
What your father called charm, you social skills, your children call emo-tional intelligence. It's all the rage and apparently leads to miraculous business successes. But can it be taught? Or is there a critical period – possibly in early adolescence – when taking an interest in others (rather than oneself and computers) enables these skills to be developed? Ever

seen those middle-aged, middle-brow, middle-managers from stores or engineering and thought how many courses they have been on to learn EQ? Being emotionally literate is important – even indispensable – among senior managers. But don't kid yourself. Only superficials can easily be taught.

5. *We have multiple intelligences*
Those who have done poorly at school or university have a vested interest in explaining away their comparative failure. Poor teaching, mystery reading difficulty, but never low ability are favoured excuses. However, thanks to the various American psychological gurus working in educational faculties people believe that there is more than just old-fashioned analytic or cognitive intelligence. There are bodily kinesthetic, creative, musical, practical, spiritual, interpersonal and intrapersonal intelligences and so on. It would be comforting to the intellectually challenged if we could show that being bad at IQ tests doesn't really count, as we are likely to be gifted in some other area. Alas for those who want their multiple intelligences explored and developed (but probably not assessed): there is little evidence to support this position. All reliable and valued IQ tests intercorrelate: bright people do better at all of them, dim people at few.

Through popular books often found in self-help sections of shops, gullible, ever-optimistic people have picked up ideas that, they believe, can fundamentally change themselves, their business and even the world. Some seek out or are recommended expert consultants to get these cures.

Whether they buy the programme they desire, as opposed to the programme they really need, is another matter.

The Icarus syndrome

The war for talent continues. The illusive high-flyers seem in short supply. Is the pool of these highly competent, creative, motivated, entrepreneurial, committed, innovative, stress-resistant (blah, blah, blah) people drying up?

The problem is not only where to find these wunder-kinds but also how to manage them. 'Creative' high-flyers are paradoxically delicate creatures who need careful nurturance. A common problem with high-flyers is that they fly too high too soon. Indeed they are prone to the Icarus syndrome.

Icarus was the son of the inventor Daedalus in the Greek myth. Both got locked up by the Cretan king Minos but, to escape, the talented and inventive Daedalus made them both wings of feathers and wax. The wise father told his son the only 'design fault' was that the wings might melt if he flew too close to the sun. Clearly the physics of the ancient Greek story tellers was not too good as the higher one flies the cooler (not the hotter) it gets. But Icarus ignored the good advice of his wise father, flew too high and due to melting of his wings crashed into the sea and drowned.

It is not clear from the myth precisely why he disobeyed his father. Was he a *sensation seeker* prone to accidents and did it out of *boredom*? Was he rather a *disobedient* child who liked to *rebel*? Was he simply *'cocking-a-snook'* at King Minos and beguiled by his own *hubris*? Was he a narcissist having passed out top of the self-esteem class of life?

We do not know. Indeed it is the function both of myths and case studies that they allow for multiple interpretations. The modern derailed high-flyer bears a canny resemblance to Icarus. But how and why are they chosen? What did the assessors miss? Or was the problem in the way they were managed?

It was probably a self-esteem problem or to use another good Greek word (and legend) *narcissism*. Narcissism is malignant self-love; overbearing self-confidence; inexplicably high self-esteem. The problem for the high-flyer is this: you probably need a great deal of self-esteem to get the job, but you need to lose some of it while on the job.

The manifestation of too much, as well as too little, self-esteem can be both a cause and a consequence of management failure. The Americans have long believed in the power and importance of self-esteem, which partly explains their self-confidence and assertiveness. It is often surprising to see, particularly, young people of very average ability look so manifestly confident. They appear all to have passed 'Assertiveness 101' but failed 'Charm 101', telling you openly and frankly about their beliefs, problems, wishes and values, as if they deserve automatic respect or are fascinating on the topic. They express little interest in others believing they are intrinsically interesting, important and love worthy.

The self-esteem industry believes that all sorts of nasty consequences follow low self-esteem: failure at school, delinquency, unemployment, crime, depression and so on. And yet we rather like the self-effacing compared to the arrogant.

Of course, one should clearly distinguish between the genuine and the fake article. There are those who are genuinely humble and meek, believing that their ability and contribution are somehow pretty average, even unworthy. The trouble with humility is that one can easily be abused by those with hubris, and be trodden upon. There is, however, deep within Anglo-Saxon culture a respect for the amateur, self-effacing person who with sheer talent wins through. It's the story of the hare and the tortoise, David and Goliath and the victory of the humble and the meek, who shall inherit the earth. Part of the appeal of the film *Chariots of Fire* depicted just such an alliance.

But people with low self-esteem seldom get into positions of power. Low self-esteem prevents risk taking, bold decision making, opportunism and openness to excitement and challenges, which are the stuff of success in business. We all need enough self-respect for healthy day-to-day functioning. We need to be sufficiently interested in, and confident about, ourselves to function well in the cut and thrust of business life.

It is those with seemingly limitless self-esteem and concomitant hubris that are the real problem. But extreme narcissists are a hazard and not that uncommon among our captains of industry. They are often people completely preoccupied with being superior, unique or special. They shamelessly exaggerate their talents and indulge in addictively boastful and pretentious self-aggrandisement. They are often mildly amusing but narcissists often possess extremely vindictive characteristics.

The psychological interpretation of unnaturally high levels of narcissism is essentially compensatory. Many business narcissists believe they have been fundamentally wronged in the past and that they are 'owed'. Their feelings of internal insecurity can be satisfied by regular adulation, affirmation and recognition. They yearn for a strong positive self-image to combat their real feelings of helplessness and low self-esteem.

One of the most frequently observed characteristics of the narcissist is capriciousness – inconsistent, erratic, unpredictable behaviour. Naturally, most psychologists see the origins of narcissistic behaviour in early childhood. The inconsistent parent (caregiver) who was attentive to all outward, public signs of achievement and success but blind to and ignorant (or worse, disapproving) of the child's personal feelings. Perhaps then, we should blame Daedalus, for Icarus's plight!

This inconsistency often leads to the young adult being confused and never developing a clear sense of who they are or establishing a coherent value system. They are 'not comfortable in their own skin'. This can and does result in a lifelong compensatory quest for full self-regard and self-assertion. The wells of the origin of the problem are both deep and murky, and passions they engender seem remorseless.

Narcissists are quite plainly dysfunctional. They fail to understand or appreciate others, be they colleagues, subordinates or clients. They often see people as sorts of possessions whose major function is as an accessory to their pursuit of fame and glory. People at work are used to reflected their glory. Do any of our current or past great business figures spring to mind at this point?

Personal and work relationships for narcissists are particularly interesting. If the narcissist's 'other half' is prepared to offer continual, unconditional, even escalatory admiration, all is well. But it requires directing all efforts, all the time, to minister to the master's needs to overcome the inner emptiness and worthlessness he/she is experiencing. Naturally, narcissists search them out because they are rare, probably equally dysfunctional, people labelled appropriately as 'complementary narcissists'. They are complementary in both senses of the word.

Many high-flyers, like Icarus, are narcissists. Indeed they find that their narcissism serves them well. They seem confident and give others confidence.

What happens to high-flyers is this: their strengths are noticed and they are fast streamed. Whichever part of the organisation they work in they tend to excel. If in marketing, they tend to be ideas and action men; resourceful and imaginative. If they are in finance they tend to be brilliant not only with figures but strategic planning. They love number tumbling and 'modelling the future'.

But they tend to be forgiven in their faults, which are overlooked. The fact that the high-flying marketing executive is undisciplined, inconsistent, poor at paper work and egocentric is ignored and downplayed. They can be unrealistic, impractical, and spend-thrift. Likewise the analytic strategists may be prone to analysis paralysis; unable to influence others and prone to building up large departments of like-minded types almost like a university department.

High-flyers, like Icarus, zoom ahead with company blessing. But their flaws, the wax wings, get noticed too late. That for which they are famous soon becomes that for which they become infamous. Known for their integrity, they can suddenly be seen as rigid, intolerant zealots. Known for their people skills, they can, just as dramatically, be labelled soft, indecisive, too tolerant of poor performance.

Alas, the very characteristics which helped one climb the greasy ladder to the top lead to the downfall. Irony? Poetic justice? No – just bad selection and management. And one wonders why Icarus was locked up in the first place.

Typical management style

Post World Cup fever has led to an interest in different management styles. Could one attribute a country's success or failure to the typical style in which people at work were managed?

Is Swedish management style somehow superior to British management style? And if all this is true, why isn't Brazil a flourishing economy?

It is interesting and natural to think about how other nations do things. So we may think of Swedes as rational realists, Danes as entrepreneurial extraverts and Norwegians as obstinate outsiders. Most Britons think of German management as controlling, even bureaucratic. They may equally think of Italian management almost as an oxymoron given the individualism and sentimentality of Italians.

But most of us know that this is patently simplistic nonsense. The best test is to read those American books instructing them how to deal with Johnny foreigner. Often their portrayal of the average English person seems pretty akin to that found in a theatrical farce. 'After high tea with the local duke one may remove one's plus fours to do a spot of old-boy networking, while simultaneously lamenting the end of the Empire.'

The British are portrayed like we used to portray Nazis in the movies. Either they were the embodiment of evil or oafish buffoons. So we are perfidious ... or quaint theme parkers. The outsider's view so simple, so ludicrous: the insider's view so complex.

It has been popular to think of typical national management style. The guru William Ouchi, over 20 years ago, tried to explain Japanese manufacturing success (of the time) in terms of six factors: lifetime employment, slow evaluation and promotion, non-specialised career paths, consensual decision making, collective responsibility and holistic concern for employees.

The whole idea of typical management style seems perfectly acceptable when it comes to others. Consider the management consultant who was recently contacted by a Swedish company deeply committed to a classic M&A with a British firm. The Swedish head of strategic planning asked for a simple but practical document on 'typical British management'.

The consultant was a little taken aback. In what sector (services, production, education)? For what size company (under 100, over 10,000)? In what time period; the 1980s, the 90s, now?

But the Swede simply repeated the request. Write us a paper on typical British management. The consultant, of course, was in a classic dilemma. Knock out some bland stereotypic nonsense of little use to anyone and trouser the dosh; or politely refuse explaining that it was essentially an impossible task.

In the jargon of social science we are talking about attribution errors. More specifically, the issue is about the perception of outgroup homogeneity and in-group heterogeneity. They are all the same but we are different. Thus it seems perfectly natural to talk about typical Swedish management but almost impossible to talk about typical British management

Yet there are dozens of books that try to describe and categorise cultures, both corporate and national. The British are individualistic rather than collectivistic. That is why they have to endure teamwork training, often conducted by sadistic ex-corporals in the 'great outdoors'. The British are also tolerant of ambiguity. We do not have a written constitution and don't worry about it. We like amateurs rather than professionals and prefer to keep things flexibly vague rather than rigidly rule-bound.

But while the above generalisations are true, there are managers and companies that demand, require and get happy team workers in a rule-bound environment.

The problem: all generalisations are misleading ... even this one!

Unlocking talent

Among the many promises made by coaches, consultants and educators is that a particular product or service will unblock or unlock some amazing hidden talent. People love to believe that they have some wonderful, but curiously unused capacity to be creative, empathic, productive, self-healing, or what-you-will.

We are, it seems, 'locked in' by external factors (rude, uncaring boss, inattentive teachers, ruthless organisation) such that our 'natural ability' cannot manifest itself. It is locked in; trapped and unable to escape.

Most of us love to believe that our academic results do not reflect our real ability. A minority believe they conned the teacher and got excellent, undeserved results which were certainly not justified by their efforts perhaps even by their ability. However, a vast majority believe that, for one reason or another (bad teachers, unfair exams, personal circumstances), their real abilities were not demonstrated. Their particular, peculiar and precious talents were locked in, and remain so.

Nowhere is 'the locked in' theory more popular than in the world of creativity. Precisely why this is the case is unclear. With very few exceptions, human characteristics are, as the statisticians say, normally distributed. This is the bell curve. A normal distribution around a mean is found for height, weight, IQ and the ability for everything from throwing a cricket ball to singing in tune. And there is no reason why it should not be true of creativity.

Perhaps the reason why people like to believe they are all above average is that there is no agreement about creativity. You have creative accountants and creative cooks: the former can be crooks, the latter no more than gastronomic terrorists. In our own little world, most of us know what creativity really is. Creative people are unusual, full stop. They have not been taught by de Bono or some other guru on the topic. They come up with unusual, radical ideas frequently and easily. The rest don't so much think as live outside the box.

Even the idea that we can be 'creative in our own way' may be a pipe dream. After all, 'idiot savants' are pretty rare. It is no doubt true that certain environments help creativity and that others hinder it. But beware the wacky ideas suggesting that a single, simple environmental modifier of creativity works. Playing music has little effect. The 'Mozart effect' was not able to be replicated. Music, smells, lights have little effect. Having someone appreciate your ideas does help, as does having explicit permission to be a bit outrageous.

People are happier and more productive in a healthy, supportive environment. Of course. But we have known for 50 years that there are limits to what social and physical conditions can do to improve performance. Personality, ability, stability and hard work are the best predictors.

Can environments inhibit performance more than they can stimulate it? This is, after all, the thesis of the 'locked in' argument. There may be some evidence that this is true. But when people are stressed, overstretched, bullied or frustrated at work, they leave, whistle-blow or simply mark time. They don't lock in their annoying talents to be discovered later.

It is true, for many people, that it may take them into early adulthood and even beyond to discover where their real talents lie. To find the round hole for your round peg is a sheer delight.

But to blame others for a talent being 'locked in' is alas little more than a mixture of wishful thinking and good marketing.

Visitors from headquarters

'I am from headquarters and I am here to help you' is a well-known lie. It is equated with 'Your cheque is in the post' and 'The restructuring will benefit everybody'.

Many centralised companies have a centre hub or administrative headquarters where all or most of the board and CEO reside. Many factors dictate where that is located geographically, but it is often a consequence of the history of the company or sheer accident.

And as companies expand first nationally, then internationally, they set up their outposts and subsidiaries. They may be exactly analogous to the imperial experience. So instead of being Viceroy of India one is General Manager: the Sub-Continent. Some organisations cut up the world by hemisphere, others by continent.

In the headquarters, those with impressive Darth Vada titles such as 'Controller of the Western Hemisphere' or 'Director of Operations: Australasia and South Pacific' or 'Head of Manpower: the Americas' have to keep an eye on their territory.

In colonial times, it was not unusual for a governor to 'go troppo'. The boredom, the drink, the dusky maidens became too much and he simply lost the plot. Another high ranking, topi wearer was dispatched to deal with the issue.

Poor communication meant it was much more difficult to keep an eye on distant outposts or semi-rebellious colonies. But this is clearly not the case with modern companies. The data on manufacturing, marketing, sales staff turn-over, gets electronically gathered and can be transmitted on a monthly, weekly or daily basis. So headquarters knows exactly what is going on.

Despite the fact that carefully chosen co-nationals are selected (and greatly rewarded) for a tour of duty at the outpost, the company often feels the need to have someone whose job is to tour the empire. They have a number of functions: some go out simply to inspire the exhausted, underpaid, bewildered and forgotten.

Sometimes, these globe-trotting executives are sent out with a mission to cut back or close the outpost. And, sometimes, the 'worldwide ambassador' role is a useful non-job, ideally suited for a manager in the departure lounge of the organisation.

1. *Inspiration*

Various types are sent for this purpose: the missionary, the messiah and the saviour. Missionaries travel to spread the faith. Faith in the product, faith in some new management technique, faith in the whole enterprise. They have read all those self-help books about self-esteem and believe all the natives need is a good dose of missionary zeal.

Missionaries exude self-confidence although when looking at their personalities and abilities, it maybe difficult to know why. They keep telling staff to believe in themselves; walk tall, fight the good fight.

When in the role of messiah, this headquarters Johnny has his way prepared. He arrives accompanied by fawning support staff, mainly to bless and praise. His presence alone is enough. He must not be troubled by trivial issues. He must be told all is well and all is successful ... and it will be. Trust him.

2. *The chop*

Again these come in various types: the accessory, the axe man, the para-trooper. When all the graphs dip downwards, the grim reaper is dispatched from headquarters to assess the real situation.

They are cold, quiet, fact finders, somewhere between a tax inspector and a mortician. They are immune to charm, flattery or colonial quaint-ness. They have the task of the bean counter, time-and-motion specialists and Hay point assessor at the same time. They want the facts: no excuses, no explanations. And they cannot be easily hoodwinked.

The paratrooper is equally uncharmable. Their job is to put backbone into the defence. They are the shock troops of the company sent in to turn around a subsidiary while there is still time. They're blunt, forceful, no nonsense sort of chaps, but have their own sort of charm.

When paratroopers fail, axe men follow. Both have seen it all before – it's their job.

3. *Displacement*

In every organisation there is the 'Manager Special-projects'. They con-duct seemingly useful but non-priority audits and comparisons and act as special advisers. They are nearly always victims of a restructuring where they survived but were emasculated. Everyone knows they are effectively powerless, pointless and patronisable.

Another version of this beast are the freeloading tourists who like the business travel; weekends in exotic resorts and expense accounts. These are the 'fact-finding mission' types, who have no clear agenda except to understand the territory and its problems. Read, play golf mid-week in the tropics and scuba dive on a really good reef. They are a real nuisance to the locals as their entertainment needs take up money, time and resources.

Occasionally the colonial manager is summoned to headquarters. This may be to explain him- or herself. They may be a sort of recalled ambassador who is meant to signal displeasure to the natives. Or he/she may be asked privately, and under a good grilling from a variety of headquarters' staff, to account for business figures in the particular company.

It is frequently worse being summoned than being visited. At least 'at home' one has the experience of support from others and familiarity. Returning to the powerhouse of headquarters with all that ritual behaviour and those self-important support staff can very easily break the confidence of a manager from the subsiduary in a far flung country.

All far flung subsidiaries develop their own culture and way of doing things. Many are faced with a serious challenge in trying to balance the seemingly rigid and impossible demands of the parent company with the requirements of the local situation. And being in the weaker position, they have to learn to read the message in who is sent and why. In this sense, the messenger is the medium of the headquarters company.

What makes a good business conference?

Business conferences are big money. Many can cost between £500 and £1000 a day per attendee. And a short day at that – of little more than four hours' chalk and talk (10.00–16.30). Senior executives are bombarded by 'invitations' to attend ' vital, crucial, state-of-the-art thinking events that are breakthroughs in achieving world class' … blah, blah, blah. Enough people attend these events to maintain a small industry that booms in the good times. Famous speakers can command easily £10,000 for a 'turn' and hundreds can be guaranteed to pitch up to hear and see their favourite guru/media person in the flesh.

Attendees for all conferences – internal and external – are encouraged to complete the 'happy sheets', namely the course evaluation forms. They provide all sorts of interesting and useful information – as well as the actual data on the overall experience.

Using feedback can help organisers justify, plan and adjust future events. They can provide useful information about what people really enjoy and why they really come: as opposed to the 'official reason' they used to justify their attendance. The following factors seem most closely related to happy sheet ratings:

Party bags: Over the years parents have realised that children's parties have to end with a party bag of assorted goodies. The idea is twofold: the bag helps the departure become easier for an excited, happy child. Also the bag fulfils the reciprocity norm – they gave a present on arrival; they get one on leaving. At conferences party bags consist of books (by the speaker), stationery with client logos, and if lucky, more frivolous and acceptable presents, even wine. It's a bit like airline bags or hotel toiletries: trivia (and relatively cheap trivia) are important.

A good party bag makes a big impact particularly because the bag is given at 'happy sheet time'.

While people believe there is a *primacy* effect at interviews (first impressions count; information that comes first is most powerful); they believe there is a *recency* effect at conferences (lasting impressions are determined at the end; best title last; importance later). The moral is simple. Charge an extra £20 and put that dosh into a really good party bag. It can make all the difference to client satisfaction.

Luncheon: Never underestimate the food and ambience. Most conferences are held at hotels and attendees have come to expect a damn good luncheon. This refers to quality, quantity, choice. Lunch (as well as the morning coffee and afternoon tea) is tangible; easy to judge. People chat about the Danish pastries when they begin; and they rabbit on about the old plates or poor vegetarian options. More recently it's about carnivore options!

For over £500 per day they expect a damn good lunch: good food expertly presented and served. They expect their quirkiness to be dealt with if they are Kosher, diabetic or vegan (ideally not all three at once) and they expect their needs to be met. Repeat purchasers may be more a function of nosh than talks.

Big names: People are attracted to conferences by famous (or infamous) people. Even if old, tired and well past their 'sell-by' date. The odd politician, guru or TV star can both attract and please an audience.

The Big Names don't have to say anything new: just be themselves. But it is important that they 'mingle at tea and luncheon'. People love to say they met Margaret Thatcher, John Harvey-Jones, Michael Porter, Esther Rantzen or Edward de Bono – even if they can't remember their names.

Occasionally the Big Name strategy backfires. They can be very disappointing indeed particularly if the blurb builds them up. Some big names have alas 'lost the plot'; others appear arrogant or lazy; some don't follow through the brief.

Big Names are expensive but they do help. But they need to be briefed, checked and monitored. They need to press the flesh; kiss babies; even appear to be sincere. A pretty tall order for some.

Network opportunities: People go to conferences to meet others. They go to bench mark. They go to buy and sell. They go to gain competitor knowledge. They go to try to find a job. A conference is a marketplace. Organisers need to know that and make sure people have sufficient 'networking opportunities'. They do this at coffee, lunch, tea. But that is not enough.

'Break out' groups are not only for the lazy presenters, they are also for networking opportunities. People study the attendee list: they like details such as email addresses. They like an opportunity to introduce themselves. Arrange times, places and activities for people to meet, sell, disclose, start an affair. It's all part of the process as they say.

Notes: These days PowerPoint presentations are de rigueur. One advantage is that it is easy to print out slides with space for people to write. Lots of people at conferences are there to steal ideas, slides, models, jokes, stories. As all students know, it is difficult to fully appreciate a lecture while trying to copy down notes.

A full set of slides is a good trophy. This must be in addition to the party bag. It often is a good rationalisation for the person to attend the course in the first place. Notes are useful because they can be used to justify and explain the course to bosses and others in the office. Despite the fact that few people ever consult their conference pack/folder ever again they like to know they have captured all the salient information. Further, it's important that all speakers provide their notes. Attendees do became very pissed-off if one speaker is 'let off the hook'. They want all the slides of all the speakers. That is value for money.

Variety: Conferences last 4–8 hours. Even the best speaker can only hold their full attention for an hour or so. Attendees like a good programme: 4–6 speakers; videos; games; break out groups. The more extraverted people are, the more they need stimulation and variety. Sitting on your bum is just not enough, however entertaining and engrossing an individual speaker is. Speakers are difficult to arrange and can be very expensive. Conference organisers would love to reduce the number of speakers to a minimum. Many are prima donnas, egocentric and demanding. And they are expensive. But getting the optimal number of speakers who use a variety of techniques to communicate is essential. It's like a mixed diet; a very varied menu.

Brilliant speakers providing new salient, information and new ideas are not enough to ensure the average business conference is well received.

The paradox for the conference organiser is that the package is as important as the content. Organisers upstage each other, literally. You need boy-band roadies to set up the venue with stage, lights and logos a day in advance, with significant cost. Attendees have come to expect theatre: somewhere between a concert and an American evangelical meeting. They come for the full experience not just the message – if there is one.

Forget the old idea that conferences are about the effective communication of ideas. Seminars and conferences are meetings at which people talk about things they should already be doing.

One should never forget that the etymology of the word seminar is semen. They need to be sexy, as we said in the 1960s, to succeed.

Wisdom in business

Inevitably certain words and concepts come in and out of fashion. Indeed, some become politically incorrect, others de rigeur. Accusing someone of having LMF (low moral fibre) or being 'a sausage short of a fry-up' is liable to get one into trouble with the HR police. Equally, neuroticism has become 'negative affectivity' and brainstorming has become 'thought showering'.

There are also new concepts in the business lexicon, some of which have a very short shelf life: reengineering, right-sizing, managing-by-walking-about. Old concepts are repackaged.

There are also some concepts which seem from another age. Stoicism seems to belong to the nineteenth century, although people may be rediscovering it. The notions of fortitude and fidelity seem terribly old-fashioned, as do manliness, civility and diligence. On the other hand, there are nu-words to reflect new concepts that may, or may not, simply be a re-heat of an old idea.

The oxymoronic concept of emotional intelligence, which can be traced back nearly 80 years, has spawned the 'discovery' of all sorts of other unlikely intelligences: spiritual intelligence, existential intelligence, naturalistic intelligence ... to name a few. Someone has recently even written a book on 'sexual intelligence' to cash in on the dual popularity of sociobiology and social intelligence.

Interest in the spiritual has seen the emergence of a very old word among business writers – wisdom. And if you really want to stump an interview panel, list wisdom as a competency. Few would disagree that wisdom in any walk of life is very desirable. They would equally agree that it is a rare attribute, and probably not trainable. There are yet to be advertisements for a 'wisdom course' run by training consultants.

In Hollywood, wisdom has to be associated with age, grey locks and a beard; a slow purring voice, short sentences from crypto-biblical sources, and talking in mini-parables. But how does wisdom show itself in the boardroom? To have a wise CEO, as opposed to an overpaid narcissistic, dictator is very desirable.

So what is wisdom in business? What are its characteristics? *First* wisdom bucks fashion: wisdom comes from a historical sense and is characterised by timeless truths. The breathless it's-got-to-be-new world of management consultants and writers is as far away from wisdom as one could get. *Second*, wisdom crosses culture as much as it crosses time. It is about an understanding of the foibles, follies and fundamentals of human nature. Language, nationality, age do have an effect but the words of the wise easily translate. *Third*, wisdom is about courage: courage to tell the truth however unpalatable at the time; courage to confront the forces of darkness often embodied in numerous political bodies; courage to let go of the past; courage to tell the emperor he is naked. Wisdom is knowing when to bend, break or disregard rules. *Fourth*, wisdom is about the poetry of simplicity. Wise people know when to speak and when to remain silent. Wisdom is about simplification; cutting the Gordian knot; articulating the obvious to those who cannot see.

It has been widely recognised that knowledge and wisdom are not the same; even quite unrelated. Knowledge is about the accumulation of facts and understanding; wisdom often about simplification. To quote Miles Kington, 'Knowledge is knowing that a tomato is a fruit. Wisdom is not putting tomatoes in a fruit salad.' Schools and universities test for understanding not wisdom: the latter may be impossible to teach. How it is achieved is a mystery. It is not necessarily related to education, though probably to intelligence. It may be acquired through hardship.

Just as people recognise that creativity and madness may be closely linked, so foolishness and wisdom may seem more synonymous than antonymous. That is, to many people, the wise thought or act may seem at first foolish. Wise people can live with contradiction and paradox.

Beware the trap of looking for prototypes. Gandhi, Mandela, Churchill: were they wise? Yes, partly. They did have a vision; they did stand their ground with immense courage; they have inspired many different groups; they did break the rules. But they also made bad decisions and very obvious mistakes.

In this sense, wisdom may not be a trait consistent over time, stable across situations. Cometh the hour; cometh the wise man. But when the hour passeth so does wisdom.

Work–life balance

One of the new business issues of our time is the so-called work–life balance. It's a curious term with possibly hidden meanings.

Work and life are not opposites. The opposite of work is leisure or non-work activities. What people mean by work–life balance is that the one has an impact on the other. Usually, work–life imbalance should be read: 'Stress and long hours at work have a deleterious effect on my private/home life, which is wrong, unfair, immoral and needs to be changed. Work has no right to affect my family and happiness.'

It has been recognised for a long time that the work/non-work relationship is dynamic and reciprocal. Activities in the one always influence the other. Indeed, both work and non-work activities are an integral part of a person's identity.

All workers have other roles outside the workplace. A manager may be a parent, spouse, sibling, sports team captain, army officer, church warden, part-time police constable, all at the same time. Some roles are more demanding than others. And some are in a sense more voluntary: one cannot easily resign from being a parent.

Further demands can change quickly and dramatically. The sick child or parent can put serious burdens on one's emotional stability and ability to concentrate at work. And being in the middle of an aggressive takeover at work can make one pretty moody at home.

But there are some findings that suggest that work–life balance may not be as 'balanceable' as some may think. First, those who are happier at the non-work activities (life) are also happier in their work activities. We all know people who move from job to job in search of satisfaction but who remain stubbornly unfulfilled and whingeing in every post. Genetic studies have shown that job satisfaction, like life satisfaction, is surprisingly heritable and therefore does not change over time within individuals.

Happiness is a stable trait. Studies have shown that those who experience great tragedy (becoming quadriplegic) or great joy (winning the lottery) return to their initial state of happiness within two to three years of the event.

What this usually means is those who are unhappy about their work–life balance are likely to remain unhappy irrespective of how the balance is adjusted. People who are unhappy and stressed outside work are likely to remain so however much work hours, responsibility and objectives are altered.

Second, there is more evidence for 'spillover' than 'compensation' in their private lives. In essence this looks at the relationship between work and leisure. Just as professional cooks may knock up soufflés in their spare time or tennis professionals play the sport to relax, we know that in general, people choose both their work and their leisure to fit their abilities, personality and values. This is 'spillover'.

People drive as they live, and all insurers know it. Further, and more importantly, their relationships at work are like their relationships out of work. People who are easy going and stress-resistant at work are the same at home; people who are agreeable, compassionate and socially aware at work are just the same out of it. In this sense, while we may *compensate* for unfulfilled needs at work with certain leisure activities, we mainly *spillover* in our leisure time because (most of us) are the same in work and out of it.

Of course one's private life affects work life and vice versa. Have a bender each weekend and work performance on Monday (if you come in) suffers. Spend all night up whether it is tending a sick child, playing bridge, watching the football or writing a novel and the sleep deprivation affects performance.

People at work can be distracted by activities outside work. And there are many common causes of distraction including addictions (drugs, drink, gambling), affairs and having two jobs or at least job hunting. Certainly work demands can be a nuisance.

The work–life lobby all concentrate on negative spillover. They stress how work makes family life difficult, problematic and unsatisfactory. But it can also do the opposite. It can support, enhance and facilitate life outside the workplace, as the redundant and unemployed soon discover.

The work–life imbalance is about conflict. Usually three types of conflict are involved: time, strain and behaviour. Time is finite: time at work cannot be spent at home. Some resent overtime, others thrive on it. When people in the public eye resign a difficult job to spend 'more time with the family', most of us know what this means. Some jobs are more demanding than others. They usually have higher rewards. They are not compulsory.

There is strain effort. Some work and family situations are prone to 'take it out of one'. The new-born baby can seriously disrupt sleeping patterns, as can jet lag from long-haul meetings. Worry over health, relationships or financial issues can make one moody at work and vice versa. But those with good coping skills apply them in both settings and those who don't, complain about balance.

And there is expected behaviour-based conflict. This means behaving differently in one setting as opposed to another. Sometimes women, but never men, ask when required to complete a personality question whether one should do it as if one is 'at home or at work'. The implication is that they are two different people and that this Jekyll and Hyde existence is tiring.

So managers beware: a call for a readjustment of work–life balance may only perpetuate the worker's problems, when a review of the fundamental fit between the person and the job may be required.

The trouble is political correctness. It takes a courageous (or unwise) manager to point out that all this work–life balance talk seems to lead to less productivity. Provide workers with good productivity statistics comparing output in different countries. This can be a sobering experience. But perhaps even more effective is to show how many jobs are being lost in work–life balance Europe and going to work–work balance Asia, where this concept is quite unknown.

Conclusion

Getting it right

Management is often a difficult, thankless if (on occasion) well remunerated task. Managers have a variety of different tasks from budgeting to PR. And most crucially they have to be good people managers.

Management like politics is the art of getting things done. But what is the essence of good man management? What skills are required? And if it is all so easy why do managers get it wrong so often?

The final section of the book will consider three things. First, three essential skills/tasks in people management. Second, why, if they are so obvious and well-known, are they either not done or done badly. Third, what are the characteristics of outstanding managers.

The necessary trio

Good management lies in three things: giving people clear, definable goals; continuous and helpful support; helpful feedback.

Goal setting

Whether it is called management by objectives or performance management, step one is about individual as well as team and function goal setting. These may be called different things:

- Individual goals
- Strategic objectives
- Key performance indicators
- Key result areas
- Measurable outcomes

The above are usually simply terminological differences favoured by different organisations for historical reasons. The task however is always the same. Individuals need to know clearly and explicitly what they should achieve. They should know what is expected of them and precisely what outcomes are effectively performance targets.

Many organisations have training courses and materials which talk about good setting. And hopefully they provide useful acronyms to help one write or recall the characteristics of good goals. Consider the following acronym: SMART.

S *Specific:* Goals should be highly specific not only to the person but to the task. Thus an individual needs a list of quite clear specific targets with respect to time, money, productivity, customer feedback. Specific means detailed and it means ideally based on previous data and trends. The opposite of specific is vague, generalised wishes rather than targets. Increase revenue by 5 per cent over the first quarter and 8 per cent over the second quarter is specific. Maximise revenue in the first part of the year is general.

M *Measurable:* You cannot manage that which you do not measure. Goals are measurable but it is surprising how poor managers are at measuring behaviour. Look at any individual's personal file stored in HR and now (hopefully) electronically stored. Even after twenty years' service what details are there on that individual's service? Often some abandoned performance management data and little else. Measurement is not easy but essential. And there are various ways of measuring individual performance.

■ *Money:* It is not difficult to measure performance in terms of profit, costs, revenue, ROI and so on. It is the 'meat and drink' of accountancy and provides sobering bottom-line data of great usefulness. Some organisations now cost meetings by working out how much people are paid by the minute and multiplying that by the time spent for each person and adding it up. More and more in business things are costed, which from a measurement point of view is most helpful. Most people only stay in business by being profitable. Managers and staff need to know, as exactly as possible, what things cost and their role in achieving targets. Most benefit from clear monetary measured targets.

■ *Time:* Time is easy to measure: how long things take to do such as answering customer letters, answering the phone, preparing sales figures. Obviously everything, well almost everything, could be done more quickly, but there is often a trade-off in quality or personal stress. An important and simple measurement can be expressed in terms of 'at month end'; 'within 5 working days'; 'at the rate of 6 customer calls per day'. To be efficient and effective means working out time cycles and the best way to do things. People work at different speeds; some tasks require more attention than others. But these can be taken into account when setting target/goal success criteria.

■ *Quantity:* Many work outputs can be counted (other than by time and money): calls taken; customers served; words written; tickets issued; operations cancelled and so on. Often organisations attempt to set up monitoring systems so that performance can be measured. The most productive worker tends to produce about 2.5 times more than the least productive worker. Goals set by quantity are essential but trade-off with quality needs to be considered.

■ *Quality:* This is much more difficult because it often introduces a much more subjective element. Quality judgements are based on personal experience, knowledge or taste. However, there is no reason to give up quality as a measurement criterion. Many producers both of products and services talk about 'quality assurance'. By this they mean trying to measure standards. Paradoxically perhaps, good quality is nearly always best assessed by poor quality. Breakages, rejects, shut-downs, and other failures are all good measures of quality. In this sense quality can be rather well measured by its opposite. Fewer failures mean high consistent quality.

■ *Customer reactions:* The customer, we have been told for 50 years, is king. They pay your salary. Customer feedback is therefore a good measure of goal accomplishment be they internal or external customers. Those not in the business of 'customer consciousness' such as internal IT or support staff often convince themselves of their excellent service until confronted by the evidence of surveys. There is however one very important feature of customer reaction that needs to be *proactive* rather than *reactive*, which is to get a good representative sample. Letters of complaint (or indeed praise) represent a very small number of people who have had bad (or good) experiences. There seems to be a small army of complaint-letter writers ever eager for some complimentary sweetener. Complaint letters are often about very specific, often unusual, incidents. The only way is to get a good survey instrument designed, which is administered to a large enough random population of customers. These may be difficult for individual measurement but very good for team or crew measurement.

■ *Electronic tagging:* With the use of cheap electronic technology it may be possible, if not always ethically desirable, to measure performance by electronic (or mechanical means). The pedometer strapped on the belt of a traffic warden reveals how far he or she walks each day. Chairs in conference centres can be designed to monitor whether someone is sitting on them. Electronic beams can measure customer flow. Video cameras can give information about customer reactions. Some electronic devices are too crude; others provide data which requires much further analysis (such as video recordings) but it seems the measurement way of the future.

The 'bottom line' on all this is simple but very important: goals must be measurable and the measures specific.

A *Achievable:* Goals set for each individual need to stretch them, challenge them. Set goals too low and one can bore individuals and fail to maximise either their potential or that of the organisation as a whole. The good managers, like the perceptive coach, know how much they can get out of any workers. They understand the abilities and motives – and limits. In many ways it is highly desirable to 'stretch' individuals particularly when they are young, eager and have much to learn. It is also important to stretch the older workers who have become sour and complacent.

The important point about achievability is that goals have to be possible not easy. Set a target unrealistically high, and therefore essentially unachievable, and you break morale. Set it too low and you encourage under performance. People differ in their aptitudes and attitudes. It is both a necessity and a skill that the manager has a good idea of the potential of the candidate. Even non-people managers can very quickly assess the technological expertise of a report. What they also need to know is how much to challenge their softer skills such as appraisal, negotiation, selling and so on.

R *Realistic:* In many ways realistic and achievable are linked. You can be realistic if the target is unachievable and vice versa.

T   *Trackable:* Every behaviour-change orientated psychologist knows that one must track behaviours. This means monitoring progress at regular intervals and plotting behaviour for the benefit of both parties. Clearly if behaviour is not measured, it cannot be tracked. Tracking gives the overall time-related pattern. It shows trends but it can also be used to highlight events that change the trends.

Flexible: The business world can be highly capricious. Bear markets can turn into bull markets very easily. Political decisions (that is, tax cuts or rises) can change the local or even global economy. This means well set goals at the beginning of the year need to be revisited to determine whether they are still apt and fully relevant. Objectives cannot be set in stone. They must reflect the ability of the individual to perform to a particular level at a particular time.

Managers must set explicit goals for individuals and teams and reward people achieving them. It is their role, once the direction has been set to provide support.

Support

It is all very well to give clear instructions and set explicit objectives but it then, of necessity, becomes the managers' job to help their report staff obtain these objectives.

There are different types of support:

- *Technical support:* People often need equipment and technology that is appropriate, up-to-date and functional to do the job. It is the managers' role to identify, source and maintain this equipment. Today nearly everyone needs computers to do his or her job.
- *Training support:* As jobs change and new equipment becomes necessary, staff need training. They also benefit from training in the soft skills of selling, counselling, negotiation. Managers need to provide timely and appropriate training.
- *Financial support:* This means more than paying the wages. All managers have a budget which may be linked to departmental efficacy. Managers, like their staff, need money to buy, fix and up-grade technology, perhaps hire in staff during very busy periods as well as use it for performance-related pay. Having poor, erratic or insufficient monetary support can be highly problematic.

■ *Informational support:* All staff need to be kept up-to-date with information about changes in trends, products, customer wishes, company plans and so on. People are worried about change and need help understanding it. Information is power: and it can empower staff.

■ *Emotional support:* Managers are responsible for morale which should never be underestimated. Morale is both a cause and consequence of productivity. It is easy to sink down on a vicious cycle where poor business results lower morale which in turn leads to further lack of success. It is partly a function of management to create virtuous cycles, that is, to help foster a spirit of optimism, commitment and loyalty which helps productivity. Loyalty is a two-way street and the manager is the embodiment of the organisation.

It is said that people join organisations but leave individual managers. Exit interviews demonstrate how some managers are almost exclusively the cause of stress. They refuse to do those man-management things which are the essence of management. They can be bullies, control freaks or absentee landlords – the very opposite of the supportive manager.

Feedback

Every coach, every psychotherapist and every teacher knows that leaning occurs fastest with accurate, regular feedback. People quite simply need to know 'how they are doing'. They need to know the criteria upon which they are being evaluated, who is doing those evaluations, and most importantly how to improve their performance.

To live in a world without feedback is to live without any knowledge of what one is doing, right or wrong. To live in a world of distorted, erratic or biased feedback may be even worse. There are various feature of good, useful feedback.

First it needs to be *reliable*. This is often achieved by either training managers to give feedback verbally and through ratings or getting more than one person to give the ratings. The enthusiasm for 360-degree ratings is a reflection of this need.

Most importantly the feedback needs to be *specific*. Too many managers duck the difficult bit of giving negative feedback. For fear that a person may get angry or upset, they give the feedback in a very anodyne or even misleading way. Numbers are less slippery than words: a 5 out of

8 rating is clearer than the feedback of moderately successful, or just above average.

Third, feedback needs to be available *regularly*. The weight watcher who stands on a scale each morning gets daily feedback on his progress. The diabetic who monitors her sugar levels through urine samples also gets regular feedback. Ideally people at work should be able to access their own feedback on performance. Call centre staff and other sales staff do. Of course it is not always easy to provide regular, specific, accurate feedback for many jobs. Hence the importance of the manager whose role it must be.

There is one other extremely important feature of feedback. That it should be *practical* and *useful*. Thus it is important to know what to do with it. To be told that one's work is below par is frustrating if it is not clear precisely what one has to do to alter that behaviour.

The role of managers like that of coaches is to 'shape' the behaviour of those they look after. They do so by giving poignant, helpful, regular feedback and advice.

Why is it not done

As we have seen, people management consists essentially of three things: setting goals, providing support and giving feedback. There is nothing new, surprising and counter-intuitive in all this. It's plain common sense. But it is surprisingly infrequently done. Why?

There are various reasons why bad managers do not set goals as described above.

- Their managers have not set goals for them, which means the cascade or trickle-down idea – that goals for each level are passed down so that the organisation is annually aligned with the business plan – simply does not happen. If you are not sure what your and your departmental goals are, it is difficult to set them for others.
- Some managers do not like to set goals for others because cumulatively they imply their own goals. If you set a target you can be evaluated against that target.
- While goal setting itself is not difficult, it is rather difficult to define success criteria. Unless management are trained they do not 'naturally' know how to measure things except in rather crude categories such as time and money.

■ There are neither rewards for, nor punishments for, not setting goals. In some organisations the whole business of performance management has a bad name and senior managers make it apparent that they do not want to 'play games'. Equally no one rewards the behaviours, save of course the workers themselves.

Why are staff not given the support they need? Managers may not have the financial means to support their staff. Or else they do not appreciate the necessity of, or need for, such things as training.

Perhaps the two types of support that are most often conspicuous by their absence are informational and emotional support. There are three reasons why people at work are not really given the information they require. First, managers themselves are kept in the dark and so they do not have the salient information to pass on. Second, they do not know what information people need; that is, they are unable to distinguish between signal and noise and give staff useful information. Thirdly, and most ominously, managers have information of crucial importance to their staff, such as a change of computer system or an M&A, but will not give it because they fear it will undermine their power and authority.

Ask average managers if they believe that their boss has some important 'secret' information which he/she has not passed on to them and 90 per cent say yes. They might or might not be right but it indicates their need to be kept informed.

Managers do not provide emotional support primarily because they do not know when or how to do it. Managers are responsible for strategy *and* morale. They need to know how to 'lift' flagging morale as well as do individual counselling for those in need. Managers need to 'look out for' the task, the group and individuals. They don't have to be caring-and-sharing training counsellors. But they do need to support their reports emotionally in time of need.

Finally, why do so many workers live in a 'feedbackless' world where they do not really know how they are doing? Most people are unhappy with their performance management system. Everybody wants feedback from those above them but nobody wants to give it. So a culture of non-adherence to the system begins. Managers and their reports conspire not to do reviews or appraisals or to do them in a cursory or perfunctory manner. Sometimes people do not receive feedback on their performance because managers have no good data on that performance. There is, in a sense, nothing to feedback, except perhaps rather vague impressionable data. Most people don't get feedback however because pusillanimous, conflict-averse managers fear giving negative feedback. Have you noticed how successful candidates are phoned up; unsuccessful candidates sent letters? It is easy to give good news; much less so bad.

Most managers have been burnt by the experience of trying to give a below-par individual some honest feedback about his/her performance. The scenario goes like this. The manager prepares his/her case with 'documentary evidence' and examples about the type of behaviour he or she is unsatisfied with. The reportee is told his/her performance is weak, and demands evidence/an example. The manager provides it. The reportee disputes it. A long argument about specific incidents in the past ensues. Both parties become emotional: angry, bitter, hurt. The experience is a failure. The manager resolves that this never happens again. And does this by avoiding the feedback activity or simply faking average for bad.

People can hear negative feedback under two conditions. First, if it's based on reliable evidence. But second, and perhaps more importantly, the person needs to know what to do to avoid this sort of feedback in the future. If you know what to do differently to receive good feedback, it is possible to hear bad feedback. Feedback is supposed to be rewarding or correcting. Its aim is to give useful insight into how one works (comparatively) and the outcomes of work.

All people in the change business know it is imperative to find ways of letting people access data on their performance. The bathroom scales give feedback on diet; the speedometer feedback on speeding, Olympic judges give feedback to divers as do judges at dog shows.

One can be taught to describe reliably and choose tea and wine such that tasters are interchangeable and the product up to standard. This is achieved by training. Judging means learning language for subtle phenomena and applying it.

At work, managers need to know both how to rate/judge/score but also how to give that information back to individuals. It is a very important aspect of their jobs and often underplayed. The ability to, and necessity of, evaluating others' performance and using this information to shape it is one of the central functions of management.

The characteristics of competent managers

There are lots of lists of this nature: the seven (or so) habits (traits) of highly successful people. Some are based on research, other not. Some use technical language, others everyday terms. The trouble with these lists is that it is unclear:

■ if the list is rank ordered from most to least important traits
■ how the traits of highly effective managers are related to each other
■ whether they are all essentially independent or statistically related
■ when the list ends. Some people want to split, others combine various traits and there seems no rationale for doing either
■ most importantly, where these traits come from: nature versus nurture; heredity versus environment. Inevitably the answer is both, but it's most important because it is an indication of how much the characteristic can be changed. That is, can it be taught/trained or has it to be selected?

The following list is not arbitrary. It is based on research though it is constantly being revised:

1. *Intelligence:* People have to be *bright enough* for the job they have to do. The more complex and varied the tasks, the brighter they have to be. The more they have to learn to keep up-to-date, the brighter they have to be. At the senior level, intelligence may be the single best predictor of success at work. And it is, alas, not trainable. Surprisingly perhaps, given the data on intelligence, it is so infrequently measured at work. Intelligence predicts both knowledge and attitude to learning.
2. *Emotional stability:* Stress at work is a given. The question is how vulnerable we are to experiencing it and how we cope with it. Less emotionally stable people are prone to anxiety, depression, hypochondria and absenteeism. Hardy, robust people are able to withstand the inevitable stresses at work. Less stable people cope poorly and have little time or energy for others.
3. *Conscientiousness:* You need to work hard to be successful at work. At times one has to come in early, stay late and take work home to complete the job on time. Some people struggle in adverse conditions and always give their best. Others give up. The work ethic is a must.
4. *Integrity:* The single feature people most want in their bosses is not competence, vision or emotional intelligence but honesty. People admire the leaders with a clear moral code and the courage to live by it. This is not a matter of zealotry but a matter of weighing up various options and acting in a way that is not dishonest.

5. *Sociability:* Great leaders work by inspiring and getting the best out of others. Some can get their staff to do almost anything through their charisma, their charm and their insight into others. They are able to be sociable and approachable. They need to know how, when and why to engage others, be they customers, staff or shareholders.

6. *Courageousness:* Good managers need courage to fail and the courage to be different. Real innovators are courageous: they have to be. It is about taking appropriate risks.

Society and technology may have changed more in the past three centuries than people. The 'secret' of great leaders has been known for ages as have the principles of good leadership. Well-known truths have to be 'repackaged' more clearly. The fact that there is essentially nothing new in the field presents, of course, a great problem for writers and publishers of management books who want impressive sales. Hence the magic-bullet and fashion-victim nature of the area. One's grandfather called it 'charm', one's father called it 'social skills', oneself 'emotional intelligence' and the next generation … 'bio-affective liability' perhaps. But it's all the same thing. And it's pretty important at work. The harder question is where it comes from: early childhood experience, biological predisposition or formal education.

Select bright, stable, motivated people with a sense of right and wrong. Teach them skills of setting goals, giving support and giving feedback. Model and reward these skills and make them the foundations of the corporate culture. Amen.